Two GREEDY ITALIANS

ANTONIO CARLUCCIO GENNARO CONTALDO

PHOTOGRAPHY BY CHRIS TERRY

Quadrille
PUBLISHING

CONTALDO

Antonio and I first met in the mid-1980s when I began collecting wild mushrooms for his restaurant in Covent Garden. After a while, he offered me a job and we gradually became close, almost inseparable, in fact. Our friendship seemed unlikely at first sight: both of us were indeed Italian, but we were so different, not least in the way we cooked! I was brought up in the south, Antonio in the north; I was and remain deeply religious, while Antonio is at best a sceptic; I am surrounded by family, while Antonio now lives alone…

Carluccio

Although we were to go our different ways for a while, both becoming successful restaurateurs and food writers, when the BBC recently asked us to work together, we were delighted! The idea of collaborating with Gennaro appeared to me initially rather complicated (usually too many cooks can spoil the broth). But then, remembering how much fun we had 15 years ago filming together for another BBC series, I recognised that we could have fun again. Our combined breadth of knowledge of Italian food could also be interesting, educational and, hopefully, entertaining for both readers and viewers alike.

INTRODUCTION

TO REDISCOVER OUR FRIENDSHIP HAS BEEN PLEASURE ENOUGH IN ITSELF, BUT WHEN COMBINED WITH REDISCOVERING OUR NATIVE COUNTRY AND ITS FOOD – HOW BOTH HAVE ENDURED, AND HOW BOTH ARE DIVERSIFYING – WE HAVE HAD THE TIME OF OUR LIVES! We returned to our home regions, one of us to the south, one to the north, experienced once more the near-forgotten sights, sounds, flavours and smells of our childhood, and shared delicious meals with old friends and family. We tasted the familiar – the simple ingredients and the wonderful flavour combinations that are so characteristic of Italy's cuisine – and, quite often, we tasted the less familiar.

For although the Italy we explored is in essence as it always was, at the same time it is changing, as everything seems to do in this modern world. Many aspects of our beloved country were different, sometimes subtly, sometimes even blatantly. Alongside the centuries' old traditions of balsamic vinegar-making, rice-growing and ham-preserving, we found an emergence of international fast-food chains and ethnic food shops, street foods and exotic ingredients. Italy was once quite insular, in attitude as well as food, but now it is home to many peoples from elsewhere who, inevitably, have had an influence on what is grown, what is imported, what is eaten and, indeed, what is enjoyed. Although both of us are dyed-in-the-wool traditionalists, we have to acknowledge that these tastes do add colour to the already colourful palette of Italian food, particularly street food. And perhaps, in time, they too will be absorbed into mainstream Italian cooking as the unfamiliar ingredients from the New World: tomato, corn, sweet pepper, aubergine and chilli, all have been….

Things were also changing in other arenas of the Italian food world, we discovered. Family life is not now as it was, and many households have fewer children, with more mothers working. As a result, family meals are shorter and less leisurely, often utilising ready-made ingredients. (And by the latter we mean dried pastas, rather than the work-intensive pastas once so lovingly made freshly at home – Italy, we hope, will never fall victim to the ready-made, chilled and frozen complete meals so prevalent elsewhere!) With women increasingly in the workplace, the traditional passing on of culinary knowledge from generation to generation has dwindled, and many young women in Italy today do not know

(nor do they care, horror of horrors to us greedier Italians) how to cook. We actually encountered a school in Emilia-Romagna which teaches young men and women to cook Italian food, something completely unthinkable in the Italy of our youth!

Although church attendance is down amongst young people throughout Italy – the epicentre of Roman Catholicism – it was encouraging for us to see how many ingredients of traditional religious practice are still part of daily life. Food and religion have always gone hand in hand in Italy, as both are so basic to everyday existence. Even one of the earliest and most distinguished of Italian cookery books came about because of the relationship between religion and food: Bartolomeo Scappi, the first celebrity chef, cooked for the Popes in the 14th century, and wrote a wonderful book, *Opera*, which went on to influence the whole of Europe. When we were on our travels, we discovered many ongoing religious celebrations – of annual feasts such as Easter and Christmas, and of saints' days – all with their own special foods. Part of the rich tapestry of Italian life, we fervently hope that these traditions will continue.

It was perhaps the potential changes in the regionality of Italian food that surprised us most. Because the country was unified so recently (in 1861), the food of Italy has always really been the food of individual regions. Inevitably, the increasing movement of people between regions – from north to south and from east to west – has blurred distinctions to a certain extent in foods and recipes of the regions. Pasta is now served all over the country, for instance, as is polenta (and one was once firmly of the south, the other of the north), and restaurant menus can now sometimes appear more national than regional in their offerings. But some things never change: the pesto of Liguria is still the best, the ham and cheese from around Parma are still unbeatable, and the combination of milky buffalo mozzarella, fresh sweet basil and ripe plum tomatoes, whether in salad or atop a pizza, continues to be at its most sublime when eaten at home in the warm south.

And the regional recipes that have most come to characterise Italian cooking – pasta, polenta, pizza, bean, offal and bread dishes – are the legacy to Italy, and the world, of the day-to-day cuisine of the Italian peasant. Known as *cucina povera*, or 'poor cooking', its dishes, once concocted from the limited ingredients available to the poor, are ironically now appearing on the tables of the rich, and are being offered at inflated prices in expensive restaurants, both in Italy and elsewhere.

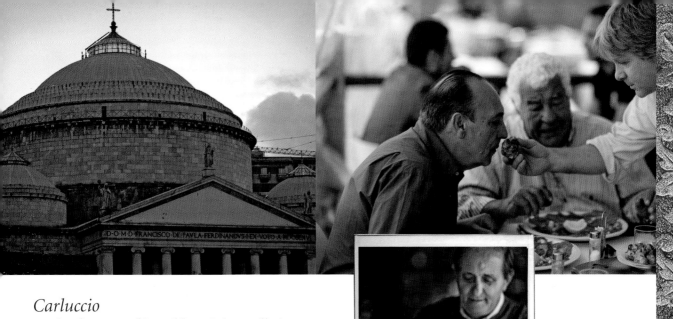

Carluccio

Both of us are of humble origin – albeit from different ends of the country – and we both enjoyed an upbringing with such food. During my childhood I marvelled at how my mother could produce wonderful dishes out of nothing. The most miraculous one was pasta e patate: a soupy concoction of pasta and diced potatoes, with the addition of garlic, olive oil and celery. It was sensational. Tastes may be evolving, but nothing can replace the original dishes that our mothers and grandmothers patiently created to achieve the maximum possible flavour and give the maximum possible pleasure.

CONTALDO

Our return to Italy turned into the most amazing journey of discovery – both of the country and its food, and of ourselves and our friendship. The food in Italy in the markets, in shops, in restaurants and in people's houses never ceased to astonish me. Italy may be gradually changing, as the rest of the world is, but the quality and abundance of produce and the love and respect shown to food are all still there and we enjoyed tasting, cooking and eating absolutely everything we encountered. After all, we are two greedy Italians!

We hope you will join us on our travels around Italy and enjoy re-creating some of our favourite recipes in this book. Buon appetito!

ANTIPASTI
STARTERS

THE WORD 'ANTIPASTO', OR STARTER, DERIVES FROM THE LATIN 'ANTEPASTUS', LITERALLY MEANING 'BEFORE THE MEAL' (not 'before the pasta' as some assume). The Ancient Romans typically started a meal with a variety of light dishes before the arrival of the main courses and, judging from historical sources, their tastes would appear to be similar to those of today – except that Italians rarely eat dormice any more…

The intention of an antipasto is to stimulate the taste-buds and the stomach just enough before more substantial dishes are served. There is a distinct art in creating a menu with starters light enough not to compromise the appetite and satiate the diner before the meal has properly started. But, in fact, Italians tend now to serve and eat antipasti only on special occasions, such as Christmas, Sunday lunches, christenings and wedding feasts. They are always readily available on restaurant menus, however, and in Piedmont, the antipasti 'capital' of Italy, you are quite often offered as many as twenty different varieties. Today's antipasti are like Spanish tapas, a snack or nibble to enjoy at any time of the day.

CONTALDO
I must admit with all the wonderful array of antipasti available in Italy, I could quite happily eat my way through all the different types and for that moment forget there is more to come…

A typical and well-loved antipasto is the traditional platter of cured or preserved meats such as *prosciutto, coppa, bresaola* and *salami* of all types: the variety is endless, and will change from region to region. There could also be some pickled and preserved items like mushrooms, olives, onions, aubergines, baby cucumbers, sun-dried tomatoes, caper berries, peppers, artichokes, along with some cheeses like mozzarella, provolone, pecorino and Parmesan. These will all be served with bread, usually *focaccia, taralli* or *grissini.*

In coastal towns, antipasti are normally seafood-based, and the choice may well include anchovies, sardines, baby octopus, mussels, clams, cuttlefish, prawns, sea urchins, tuna, herring and bottarga (eggs of tuna or mullet). Fish such as whitebait are often deep-fried, and *fritelle di baccalà* (salt cod fritters) are especially popular in the south on Christmas Eve. Vegetables are also deep-fried, and these include cauliflower, sun-dried tomatoes and fresh artichoke fritters, as well as *olive ascalone,* deep-fried large olives stuffed with meat or tuna. Salads are popular, too. Indeed, you can serve practically anything you like as an antipasto, but four or five items at one time should be enough.

CONTALDO

1 large **courgette**, thinly sliced
3 tbsp **extra virgin olive oil**, plus extra for oiling and drizzling
salt and freshly ground **black pepper**
1 **garlic clove**, very finely chopped
10 **mint leaves**, plus extra for garnish
2 tbsp **white wine vinegar**
4 slices of good **country bread**, toasted
4 **cherry tomatoes**, sliced

SERVES 4

CROSTINI DI ZUCCHINI ALLA SCAPECE
Crostini with Minted Courgettes

'Alla scapece' *in southern Italian dialect term, thought to come from Spanish, for a vegetable (usually courgette) marinated in a sweet-sour dressing. The courgettes are normally fried and then marinated with fresh mint, but, to make the recipe healthier, I have lightly roasted them first and have used them as a topping for* crostini – *though they work very well as a starter or a canapé to serve with drinks at parties as well. I dedicate this recipe to my nephew Mario, who gave me the idea while I was researching* crostini *recipes for this book!*

Preheat the oven to 200°C/Gas 6.

Place the courgette slices on a lightly oiled baking tray and sprinkle with a little salt. Put in the oven and cook for 10 minutes, turning halfway through, until golden.

Meanwhile, combine the olive oil, garlic, mint leaves, vinegar and a little pepper in a bowl. Add the cooked courgette slices to the dressing and leave to marinate for 5 minutes. Drizzle a little extra virgin olive oil over the toasted bread and top with the courgettes, cherry tomato slices and mint leaves.

2–3 large **courgettes**
salt
100g **Gorgonzola**, roughly
   chopped into chunks
6 **sun-dried tomatoes** in oil,
   finely sliced
a bunch of **basil** leaves

MARINADE
4 tbsp **extra virgin olive oil**, plus
   extra for oiling
1 large **garlic clove**, finely
   chopped
freshly ground **black pepper**

MAKES ABOUT 16 INVOLTINI

CONTALDO

INVOLTINI DI ZUCCHINI
Roasted Courgette Rolls

*This is a really tasty starter, which is ideal to serve at parties with
a glass of Prosecco. It is a modern antipasto, combining a typically
southern Italian vegetable with a classic northern cheese.*

Preheat the oven to 180°C/Gas 4.

Combine the marinade ingredients in a small bowl and set aside.

Cut the courgettes lengthways into slices about 5mm thick. Arrange
the slices on a plate, sprinkle with salt and leave to rest for 40 minutes,
until they have exuded some liquid and are soft.

Pat the courgette slices dry with a tea towel, place on a lightly oiled
baking tray and brush with some of the marinade. Roast the courgettes
in the oven for 10–15 minutes, until the edges begin to golden. Turn
the courgette slices over, brush with the remaining marinade and cook
for a further minute. Remove from the oven and leave to cool.

Place a few pieces of the Gorgonzola, a couple of slices of sun-dried
tomato and a leaf or two of basil at one end of each courgette slice and
roll up. Arrange on a serving dish and garnish with basil leaves.

500g fresh **porcini** (cep)
8 tbsp **extra virgin olive oil**
juice of 1½ **lemons**
salt and freshly ground **black
  pepper**
4 tbsp finely chopped **garlic
  chives** or ordinary chives

SERVES 4

Carluccio

INSALATA DI PORCINI
Porcini Salad

*Italians eat their porcini (ceps) raw, with great pleasure, as soon as
the season starts (in early summer). To be eaten in this way, they
have to be very firm, not too old, and small in size. If you can't find
porcini you can always substitute very small, firm, closed button
mushrooms instead.*

Brush the mushrooms clean and slice very finely.

Arrange the mushroom slices on a platter. Drizzle over the oil first,
then the lemon juice, and season with salt and pepper to taste.
Scatter with the chopped garlic chives and serve immediately.

MUSHROOMS AND TRUFFLES *Carluccio*

When you talk about wild fungi in
Italy the first words that come to
mind are *porcino* and *tartufo* (cep and
truffle). Everyone expectantly awaits
the appropriate season for collecting
them wild in the woods, cooking and
preserving them, and the Alps and
Appennines offer wonderful hunting.

My mycological career has lasted
for more than 65 years, and I can now
recognise and safely pick about 200 of
the more than 200,000 recognised species
of mushrooms. In this huge number,
however, the majority of fungi don't look
like mushrooms. The truffle is one such,
growing in symbiosis with the roots of
certain trees. The white truffle of Alba is
the most precious and can only be found
with the help of a specially trained dog.
They can cost up to £3,000 per kilo. The
black Périgord truffle is less valuable, but
still commands high prices.

250g dried **chestnuts**
salt and freshly ground **black pepper**
150g unsalted **Alpine butter**, chilled and cut into small cubes

SERVES 4–6

Carluccio

CASTAGNE AL BURRO
Buttered Chestnuts

This antipasto is a revival of an old cucina povera *recipe, typical of the Aosta Valley in the north of Italy. Chestnuts were used there in many different ways – as a basic porridge (the antecedent of polenta), even as a flour for bread and pasta. In my opinion this is the richest antipasto you may ever have, but it is delicious – so long as you eat it in moderation…*

Place the chestnuts in a bowl, cover with cold water and leave to soak for 12 hours.

Drain the chestnuts, put in a large pan and cover with lightly salted water. Bring to a simmer and continue to cook until the chestnuts are soft, but not falling apart, about 1½ hours. The chestnuts will turn brown as they cook.

Drain well, and serve hot, sprinkled with pepper and cubes of cold butter. The idea is to eat the chestnuts warm with the cold butter – do not wait for the butter to melt.

WILD FOOD *Carluccio*
The Italians love gathering wild food, some collecting for themselves, some for selling to specialist shops. It starts in spring when you see people in fields armed with knives and plastic bags, collecting young dandelion leaves for a salad. Then it is wild garlic, and *bruscandoli* (wild hops, which taste wonderful in a frittata). Wild asparagus and wild rocket are also tasty (as a boy I picked wild rocket from the side of the railway). The season continues with wild sorrel for risotto, and the first mushrooms, while summer is fabulous, with elderflowers and later berries, wild hazelnuts and apples. Autumn brings walnuts, chestnuts and more mushrooms to be preserved.

Many Italians also hunt for game – in the past this was a natural way of getting meat on the table. Personally, I am not a hunter; Gennaro is, and I get my game from him.

500g **beef tomatoes**
500g **buffalo mozzarella**
salt and freshly ground **black pepper**
a pinch of dried **oregano**
a handful of **basil leaves**
100ml **extra virgin olive oil**

SERVES 4

CONTALDO

INSALATA CAPRESE
Mozzarella and Tomato Salad

Probably one of the most famous of Italian dishes, this is also very simple. In restaurants throughout the world, it is often served as a side dish (and can be done very badly), but Italians eat it as a starter, perfect on hot days. The dish is called 'caprese', because it comes from Capri, in the Campania region where, of course, the very best buffalo mozzarella, beef tomatoes and basil come from.

Slice the tomatoes and mozzarella and arrange on a serving dish.

Season with salt and pepper, sprinkle over the oregano and basil leaves, drizzle with the oil and serve with some good bread.

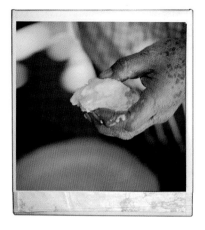

MOZZARELLA CHEESE
CONTALDO

Mozzarella is a soft, fresh, un-aged cheese originating in the Campania region. It is now produced worldwide, and its popularity over the last 30 years or so has grown enormously. Mozzarella is made not only from buffalo's milk but also from cows' milk. Different types are produced. A harder, aged version is sold in blocks with a longer sell-by date, which is usually used in cooking (in *parmigiane* and on pizzas). The soft, more perishable variety is sold packed in some of its own whey, usually in a ball shape (often tiny, as *bocconcini*). These are best eaten raw.

A smoked mozzarella (*affumicata*) is also available. Scamorza cheese is a close relation of mozzarella, but is firmer in texture and is sold in a moneybag shape. It can be used in cooking, as can its smoked version, *scamorza affumicata*.

PANZANELLA AGLI ORTAGGI IN AGRODOLCE
Sweet and Sour Bread Salad

This is a twist on the traditional panzanella, *a classic* cucina povera *dish which is usually made with tomatoes and bread. In this recipe I have used a variety of vegetables and cooked them with sugar and vinegar to give them an extra kick! If you can find* fresella, *the Pugliese hard double-baked bread, in your local deli, I suggest you use it, otherwise good country bread slowly cooked in the oven will do. This dish can be served warm or cold and, if you increase the quantities, makes a lovely light lunch.*

Blanch the carrot and celeriac or celery strips in boiling salted water for 5 minutes. Drain well and set aside.

Heat the olive oil in a large frying pan, add the anchovies and cook, stirring, until they have almost dissolved into the oil. Add the shallots and garlic and sweat over a medium-high heat until softened. Add the peppers, aubergine and courgette strips and cook, stirring, over a medium heat for a couple of minutes, then stir in the thyme leaves, sugar and vinegar, and season with salt and pepper. Add the blanched carrot and celeriac to the pan – taking care not to squash and break them – cover with a lid and cook for 5 minutes. Remove the lid and cook for a further 5 minutes, until all the vegetables are tender. Remove from the heat and set aside.

Break the *fresella* or toasted country bread slices into bite-size pieces and assemble in a serving dish. Top with the vegetables, scatter over the basil leaves and drizzle with a little oil. Serve immediately.

1 small **carrot**, peeled and cut into julienne strips
120g **celeriac** or celery, peeled and cut into julienne strips
125ml **extra virgin olive oil**, plus extra for drizzling
2 **anchovy fillets**
2 **shallots**, finely sliced
1 **garlic clove**, finely chopped
½ **red pepper**, deseeded and cut into julienne strips
½ **yellow pepper**, deseeded and cut into julienne strips
½ **aubergine**, cut into julienne strips
1 small **courgette**, cut into julienne strips
2 sprigs of **thyme**, leaves only
2 tsp **sugar**
3 tbsp **white wine vinegar**
salt and freshly ground **black pepper**
100g *fresella*, softened with water, or toasted country bread
8 **basil leaves**, roughly torn

SERVES 4

2 tbsp **extra virgin olive oil**,
  plus extra for oiling
2 **garlic cloves**, finely chopped
4 large fresh **sardines**, cleaned,
  scaled and butterflied by the
  fishmonger
2 tbsp **oregano**, plus some leaves
  for garnish
2 tbsp dried **breadcrumbs**
  (see page 154)
salt
juice of 1 **lemon**

SERVES 4

Carluccio

SARDINE IN TORTIERA
Baked Sardines

When you are in a fish market such as Salerno – or any other market throughout coastal Italy – the sardines seem to jump out at you, they are so fresh, begging to be cooked! Whenever you find such fresh fish (Italians might use anchovies instead) one of the best ways to cook them is in tortiera (baked in a special tray). If you are able to find anchovies, by all means use them; the method is exactly the same, you will just be working on a much smaller scale.

Preheat the oven to 200°C/Gas 6.

Lightly oil a large baking dish and sprinkle with the chopped garlic. Layer the butterflied sardine fillets on top like roof tiles. Sprinkle over the oregano, breadcrumbs and salt to taste, then drizzle with the oil.

Bake in the preheated oven for about 10–12 minutes. Sprinkle with lemon juice, garnish with a few fresh oregano leaves and serve with good bread.

12 **quail's eggs**
80g tinned **tuna** in oil, drained and very finely chopped
2 tsp salted **capers**, soaked in water for 10 minutes, drained and finely chopped, plus some extra whole to garnish
1½ tbsp **mayonnaise**
salt and freshly ground **black pepper**

SERVES 4

Carluccio

UOVA DI QUAGLIE RIPIENE
Stuffed Quail's Eggs

I actually invented this recipe for hen's eggs, but I like the prettiness and delicacy of this alternative version, which is very good served as one of several antipasti, as a canapé, or even given to children when they come home from school, as a merenda (snack).

Place the eggs in a small pan of water, bring to the boil and cook for 12 minutes. Add the eggs to a bowl of cold water to cool before peeling (this is easiest to do with the eggs still submerged in the water).

Cut the eggs in half lengthways. Carefully take the yolk out of each half gently and arrange the egg whites on a plate. Put the yolks in a bowl together with the tuna, capers and a tablespoon of the mayonnaise and mix together. Season with a little salt (being careful as the capers may be salty) and pepper.

Using your hands, take a little of the egg yolk mixture, about 1 teaspoon, and roll it into a little ball. Put into the cavity of a half egg. Do this with all the remaining half eggs (be warned, this job is fiddly!).

When all are finished, spoon over a little of the remaining mayonnaise. Quarter a few whole capers and place on top of each half egg for garnish. *Buon appetito!*

750g fresh *baccalà* (salt cod)
50g **plain flour**
2 **eggs**, beaten
olive oil, for shallow-frying (or
   a mixture of olive and seed oils)
freshly ground **black pepper**
juice of 1 **lemon**

SERVES 4

Carluccio

FRITELLE DI BACCALA
Salt Cod Fritters

In Italian street markets, the appetites of shoppers are roused by the smell of frying fish that permeates the whole area. The most traditional are frittelle di baccalà *(salt cod fritters), which are a common street food throughout the whole of Italy and are typically eaten on Christmas Eve in the south. Baccalà can be bought from a good fishmonger or Portuguese delicatessen, but if you are finding it difficult to get hold of, you can always substitute it with whitebait, anchovies or sardines. In Naples they serve a local tomato sauce with these fritters. I prefer them without, but you could always accompany them with a lovely tomato and basil salad, if you wish.*

Cut the *baccalà* into steaks about 7 x 10cm and place in a large bowl with plenty of cold water. Soak for 48 hours, changing the water three or four times. Do this soaking skin-side up, as this enables the salt to fall to the bottom of the bowl.

In another bowl, mix the flour and eggs to make a light batter. Pour enough oil into a medium-sized frying pan to cover the base generously, and heat until it just starts to smoke.

Dip the steaks in the batter and fry in the hot oil for 5–6 minutes on each side (you may need to do this in batches).

Drain on kitchen paper and serve hot with a sprinkle of pepper and a squeeze of lemon juice.

REGIONALISM

IN ONE SENSE, THERE IS NO SUCH THING AS 'ITALIAN' FOOD, rather there is only 'regional Italian' food. For, until as recently as 1861, when the country was united, Italy consisted of many separate and autonomous kingdoms and dukedoms, each with their own languages, customs and, of course, their own individual foods.

Geography and climate play a major part in this: in the Alpine north of the country, whole valleys can be cut off from their neighbours, as can communities down the length of the Appenines. The life of a fisherman in the south, in a Mediterranean climate, will differ dramatically from that of a sheep farmer in the Südtirol, with its hard winters. Because of geographical isolation, ideas and produce have not circulated and thus, in the 150 years since unification, the country, now divided into twenty regions, has retained its regionality despite that nationhood. For instance, if you ask an Italian where he is from, he will tend to name his town before he even mentions Italy! In Piedmont, where I was raised, this sense of allegiance goes even further: the first loyalty is to family, then to neighbourhood, then to local town followed by region. In the north, this love of place is called *campanalismo,* which roughly translates as 'pulling together to defend the bell-tower'.

And that defence was vital in the past, because the history of Italy is rich in conflict, between towns, between regions, even between countries. Throughout history, Italy was invaded many times, and by many nations, and various influences are still apparent in regional customs, language and, again, food.

Piedmont's antipasti are legion, due to the influence of French *hors d'oeuvres* (it was ruled by Savoy for many decades). In the north-east, the Germanic countries have had an influence: the *fonduta* of the Val d'Aosta is the equivalent of the Swiss fondue, the Lombardan *bresaola* (air-dried beef) of the Swiss *Bündnerfleisch*. In Trentino-Alto Adige, Veneto and Friuli-Venezia Giulia you find the very un-Italian *knödeln* (dumplings), *crauti*, *speck*, *strüdel* and *gulasch*. Some Italian villages in the east speak German, French is spoken in the west and, in many cases, they opt for a patois that is impenetrable to everyone!

Regionality is still alive in Italy today, in all senses, although inevitably it is changing: with globalisation, with the introduction of foreign food multinationals and with an increased ease of travel and with immigration. These immigrants are not only from other countries: since the 1950s there has been an influx of southerners in the north of Italy. They may seek northern jobs and wealth, but they still wish to retain their southern identity, in food certainly, and to this end, large container lorries arrive in the north weekly – laden with tomatoes, sweet peppers, aubergines, garlic, lemons, mozzarella and pecorino. Associations have been formed to protect traditional regional ideas (such as Slow Food, for instance), while some stalwarts are so vehemently against change that occasionally this sense of *campanilismo* can seem quite hostile to the outsider.

The concept of local 'wars' continues today – but mainly in terms of who produces the best white truffles or who makes the best salami – as well as on and off the football field, of course! The numerous *palii* (bareback horse races) held in Piedmont commemorate the more serious rivalries of the past. The *palio d'Asti*, one of the oldest in Italy, began when the Astigiani fought back against the trade sanctions of nevarby Alba. They devastated Alba's vineyards and orchards and, on Alba's patron saint's day, raced their horses around the city walls as a symbolic act of defiance. This race has been re-created ever since in Asti, and now riders from different wards of the city and outlying villages vie with each other for the prize.

Although I devoutly hope that Italy's regional cuisines will never be lost, I think it inevitable that they will change in some way. After all, many of what we think of as Italy's most characteristic foods and ingredients – pasta, rice, maize, peppers and tomatoes – were actually introduced from elsewhere. Centuries ago, the Italians took to them, adopted them and made them their own. It is not beyond the bounds of possibility that the new ingredients and ideas coming in, by whatever means, may too be accepted and absorbed in turn. Perhaps this novelty could be seen then, not as threatening, but as enriching…

Carluccio

Carluccio

600g **rose veal fillet**, coarsely minced (or chopped with a very sharp knife)
3 tbsp **extra virgin olive oil**
salt and freshly ground **black pepper**
1 tsp **truffle oil**
4–6 **flat-leaf parsley sprigs** or fennel fronds, finely chopped, plus extra to garnish
juice of 2 small **lemons**

SERVES 4–6

INSALATA DI CARNE CRUDA AL PROFUMO DI TARTUFO
Truffled Raw Meat Salad

This Piedmontese meat salad, the Italian equivalent of the French steak tartare, is one of the most decadent poor man's dishes I know – traditionally being made with a bit of veal (or beef), along with a white truffle, perhaps, that the farmer couldn't sell. I've substituted truffle oil here in place of white truffle for us lesser mortals, and if you wanted to you could also garnish this with a slice of summer truffle on top as decoration. Serve as part of an antipasti spread.

Put the minced or chopped meat in a bowl and add the olive oil, salt and pepper, truffle oil, chopped parsley or fennel and the lemon juice. Mix together with your hands, and taste for seasoning.

Divide this mixture between the plates, piling it in the centre. Top with a sprig of parsley or fennel. Serve with bread or *grissini* (breadsticks).

CONTALDO

ANTIPASTO DI MARE
Seafood Antipasto

This is a classic antipasto found on the menus of most coastal restaurants in Italy. You can use a variety of shellfish, molluscs and even fresh raw fish such as bream, if you like, but whatever you choose, make sure you buy the freshest seafood you can. Here I give a traditional version, but with the addition of some preserved peppers and baby gherkins to give your taste-buds that extra kick!

Bring a medium-sized saucepan of water to the boil, add the baby octopus and simmer for about 10 minutes, until tender. Remove from the heat and drain.

Clean the mussels and clams by washing them in plenty of cold water, scrubbing them well and removing any beards. Place in a saucepan with the wine, cover with a lid and cook over a high heat for a few minutes, shaking the pan from time to time. When the shells have opened, remove from the heat and leave to cool. Discard any that have not opened.

Blanch the prawns in boiling salted water for a couple of minutes. Remove from the heat and drain.

Remove the meat from the mussels and clams (keeping a few in their shells for garnish) and discard the empty shells. Place all the seafood in a large bowl and set aside.

Combine the olive oil, lemon juice, garlic, chilli (if using), capers, parsley, salt and pepper in a bowl and mix well. Pour over the seafood, toss to combine and leave to marinate for about 30 minutes. Arrange on a serving dish with the slices of pepper and the baby gherkins.

12 **baby octopus**, cleaned
20 **mussels**
28 **clams**
50ml **white wine**
12 **king prawns**, shelled
8 tbsp **extra virgin olive oil**
juice of 1 **lemon**
1 **garlic clove**, finely chopped
½ **red chilli**, finely chopped (optional)
1 tsp **capers**
a handful of **parsley**, finely chopped
salt and freshly ground **black pepper**
3 slices **preserved red pepper**
3 slices **preserved yellow pepper**
8 whole baby **gherkins**

SERVES 4

400g **beef fillet**
6 tbsp **extra virgin olive oil,** plus
   extra for drizzling
2 tbsp **lemon juice**
salt and freshly ground **black
   pepper**
1 small **fennel bulb**, very finely
   sliced
4 handfuls of **rocket leaves**
50g **pecorino**, finely shaved
2 tsp grated **orange zest**

SERVES 4

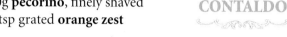

CONTALDO

CARPACCIO DI MANZO CON FINOCCHIO E PECORINO
Beef Carpaccio with Fennel and Pecorino

Although carpaccio *is not a centuries' old Italian dish, this
restaurant favourite has become a classic worldwide. The original*
carpaccio *was made with beef (as is mine), though a 'carpaccio'
has now come to mean any ingredient sliced very thinly and can be
made of fish, vegetables, even cheese. A lot of people can be put off
by raw meat, but if you buy really good-quality fillet of beef from
a trusted butcher and ask him to cut it really thinly you will eat
something that tastes wonderful and is also incredibly healthy.*

If your butcher has not already done so, cut the beef into very thin
slices against the grain and place between two sheets of clingfilm. Beat
gently with a meat tenderiser until you get very thin slivers. Arrange
on a large serving dish or divide between four individual plates.

Mix together the olive oil, lemon juice, salt and pepper and drizzle
over the meat slices. Leave to marinate for 5 minutes.

Scatter over the fennel slices, rocket, pecorino and orange zest and
drizzle with a little more oil. Serve immediately.

PRIMI
FIRST
COURSES

THE *PRIMO* (FIRST COURSE) IN ITALY USUALLY CONSISTS OF ONE OF PASTA, RISOTTO, GNOCCHI, POLENTA OR SOUP, BUT THIS VARIES FROM REGION TO REGION. Antipasti are often only for special occasions, so the *primo* on the whole acts as the opener to the meal, and is often the most important part of it. Traditionally the main meal in Italy was at lunchtime when the *primo* was a must, followed by the *secondo* (main course). This is changing now among young urban Italians, who can no longer return home for lunch, but still holds true in smaller towns and villages and among the older generation. A majority of Italians would still consider a meal incomplete without this course, and often it is now being substituted for the main course proper.

Carluccio
The sexiest dish for impromptu guests is spaghetti aglio, olio e peperoncino – *garlic, oil and chilli – which takes 5–6 minutes to make, and can be consumed at any time you feel hungry!*

Soups are very much part of the Italian diet, and vary regionally (as does everything else!). Some are light broths with small *pastina* (tiny pasta shapes) added, while others are more substantial and are based on vegetables, such as the classic minestrone or various *zuppi di fagioli*. These can be a meal in themselves, an ideal lunch if accompanied by good bread, and sprinkled with Parmesan and olive oil.

Fresh pasta is still made at home, but because it requires a little work, this is probably limited now to Sundays and times of festivity. Most Italians will have a good choice of dried pasta in their larders, ready to be turned into a quick *primo* or complete meal (with a salad). Some of the sauces can be quickly prepared while the pasta is cooking, though many, such as a meat-based bolognese, will take very much longer.

Risotto is another favourite, but you must use the correct rice variety, one that can absorb water at the same time as exuding starch while cooking, so that it achieves the desired creaminess and yet still be *al dente* as the Italians like it. Polenta, once an ingredient of *cucina povera* (see pages 150–151), has been rediscovered and is offered in almost every restaurant accompanied by a *ragù* of meat, offal or mushrooms, as are gnocchi – the delicious dumplings most commonly made with mashed potato, flour and egg.

In the old days, pasta and these other *primi* carbohydrates were dishes of the poor. They would eat just that, a generous portion which would have to last them all day. Nowadays, restaurant portions are quite minimal because they are served as part of a larger meal. How things have changed. The food of the poor has become a delicacy!

Carluccio

ZUPPA DI CARCIOFI CON GNOCCHI DI POLLO
Artichoke Soup with Chicken Dumplings

This is a lovely, delicate soup which can be eaten in smaller quantities as a starter, but can be served in more generous portions as a main course, simply with some bread. The little dumplings, or knödeln in German, remind me of those cooked in broth in the Alto Adige. As long as all bones and skin have been removed, they can also be made with leftover cooked chicken.

Remove the tough outer leaves from the artichokes, then cut in half and remove any choke. Cut the remaining artichoke into thin slices.

Pour the stock into a large pan and add the artichokes, potatoes and celery. Bring to the boil, lower the heat and simmer for about 15–20 minutes, until the potato is soft and the artichoke slices are tender, but still intact. Season with salt and pepper to taste.

Meanwhile, make the chicken dumplings. Put all the ingredients into a bowl, and, using a hand blender, whiz into a paste. Season to taste. Shape the chicken mixture into quenelles with two teaspoons, or make into little balls using your hands. Add to the hot soup and cook for a further 5–6 minutes.

Pour the soup into bowls, dividing the artichoke slices and chicken dumplings evenly. Sprinkle with grated Parmesan and serve.

4 small **globe artichokes**
1.25 litres **chicken stock**
  (see page 38)
150g **potatoes**, peeled and finely
  diced
2 tbsp finely chopped **celery**
salt and freshly ground **black
  pepper**
freshly grated **Parmesan**, to serve

CHICKEN DUMPLINGS
1 boneless **chicken breast**,
  skinned and very finely minced
1 tbsp chopped **flat-leaf parsley**
½ **garlic clove,** very finely
  chopped
a small pinch of freshly grated
  nutmeg
30g **fresh breadcrumbs**
1 **egg**, beaten
10g **Parmesan**, freshly grated

SERVES 4

about 1 litre good **chicken stock** (see below) or vegetable stock
100g **garlic**, about 20–30 cloves, peeled and finely diced, plus one clove left whole
3 small **potatoes**, peeled and very finely diced
salt and freshly ground **black pepper**
4 slices **ciabatta bread**, toasted
2 tbsp good **olive oil**
60g **Parmesan**, freshly grated

SERVES 4

Carluccio

ZUPPA DI AGLIO
Garlic Soup

You will find this soup all over the world, a classic of farmers and peasants who might have nothing else to cook. Think of sopa de ajo in Spain and soupe de l'ail in France. For the best flavour, you need a very good chicken (or vegetable) stock, and young fresh garlic.

Put the stock in a large pan, and add the diced garlic and potato. Bring to the boil, lower the heat and simmer for about 20 minutes. Leave to cool a little, then process in a food processor or blender until smooth. Season with salt and pepper to taste.

Meanwhile, cut the remaining garlic clove in half and use to rub the toasted bread slices. (Do this gently as the raw garlic has a very strong flavour!) Drizzle the toast with a little olive oil, then put each slice on the bottom of a soup plate. Pour the hot soup on top, and sprinkle with the grated Parmesan just before serving.

BRODO DI GALLINA O CARNE
Chicken or Beef Stock

To make a chicken or beef stock, put about 1kg chicken legs and wings or 500g stewing beef and some bones, in a saucepan with water to cover (perhaps 2 litres) along with a carrot, 2 celery sticks, an onion, halved, 2 bay leaves and a handful of black peppercorns. Bring to the boil, then turn the heat down, and skim off the froth. Simmer, uncovered, for 2–3 hours for beef, slightly less for chicken. Strain and remove the fat. Chill and use as required within 4–5 days, or freeze.

1.6 litres **water**
500g fresh **borlotti beans** (shelled
    weight)
500g ripe **tomatoes**, deseeded
    and roughly chopped
1 **celery stalk**, finely chopped
5 tbsp **extra virgin olive oil**
¼ tsp dried **oregano**
1 **garlic clove**, finely chopped
a handful of **parsley**, roughly
    chopped
salt and freshly ground **black
    pepper**

SERVES 4

CONTALDO

ZUPPA DI BORLOTTI FRESCHI ALLA MARUZZARA
Borlotti Bean Soup

Fresh borlotti beans with their pretty reddish-purple colour are a welcome sight in the local markets in early summer, although only for a short time: if you do come across them in season, please buy them! Dried borlotti beans, however, are just as good and readily available, just follow the packet instructions for soaking in advance (you may also need to allow a little extra cooking time). Alla maruzzara refers to the fishermen who traditionally would take this soup with them on their night-long expeditions.

Pour the water into a large saucepan, add the borlotti beans and cook for about 40 minutes. Add the tomatoes and celery and continue to cook until the beans are tender, about a further 20 minutes.

Check that there is plenty of liquid in the soup, otherwise add some more. Stir in the oil, oregano, garlic and parsley, season with salt and pepper and serve with some good toasted bread.

800g **Savoy cabbage**, chopped
salt and freshly ground **black
  pepper**
1.5 litres **chicken stock** (see page
  38) or vegetable stock
175g leftover or stale **white
  bread**, baked until dry
220g **Taleggio cheese**, sliced
80g **Parmesan**, freshly grated
75g **unsalted butter**
2 **garlic cloves**, sliced

SERVES 4

Carluccio

ZUPPA DI CAVOLO CANAVESANA
Canavese Cabbage Soup

*Cabbage is a widely grown, humble vegetable that can be used
in a multitude of ways. In Italy there are many different types of
cabbage soup and this one comes from Canavese, in Piedmont. My
mother would regularly make it in winter – cheap, nutritious and
wholesome, it was her solution to the problem of feeding a ravenous
family of six. When the day came she would ask me to pull up a
cabbage. Many is the time I had to dig through a blanket of snow,
under which I would find a perfect vegetable; crisp, bright in colour,
and very, very cold!*

Put the cabbage in a pan and cover with lightly salted water. Bring to
the boil, lower the heat and simmer for 30 minutes, until the cabbage
is very soft. Drain well.

Bring the stock to the boil in a pan.

In a separate large pan, place a layer of cabbage, then a layer of dried
bread pieces, Taleggio slices and Parmesan. Layer up like this as many
times as you can, until all the ingredients have been used.

Using a wooden spoon, make a hole in the layered ingredients and
fill it with a little of the boiling stock, so that the stock reaches all the
bread, which will absorb it and soften. Pour over as much hot stock as
is needed to just cover the ingredients and place over a gentle heat to
keep warm.

Melt the butter in a small pan and fry the garlic gently until just
beginning to colour. Pour this over the top of the soup and mix
everything together. (It may not look pretty, but it tastes delicious!)
Serve immediately.

3 tbsp **extra virgin olive oil**

4 slices **pancetta** or bacon, finely chopped

1 large **onion**, finely chopped

1 large **potato**, peeled and finely chopped

300g **stinging nettle tops**, stems trimmed off and discarded

100g **rocket leaves**, roughly chopped

1 litre **vegetable stock**

3 tbsp grated **Parmesan**

SERVES 4

CONTALDO

CREMA DI ORTICA
Nettle Soup

Stinging nettles are widespread, free and abundant in almost every type of environment, as well as being a good source of vitamins and iron. I like to collect nettles in spring when the leaves are tender and at their best; in summer the leaves become coarser and are bitter to eat. When collecting and preparing, I strongly recommend you wear protective gloves!

Heat the oil in a saucepan, add the pancetta or bacon and fry until crispy, then remove and set aside. Add the onion to the pan and cook gently until soft, then add the potato, nettles, rocket and stock. Bring to the boil, lower the heat and simmer, covered, for 30 minutes.

Remove from the heat, stir in half the Parmesan and whiz in a blender until smooth. If the soup has cooled during this process, return to the pan and reheat as necessary.

Divide between four soup bowls and sprinkle over the remaining Parmesan and the pancetta or bacon. Serve with toasted bread.

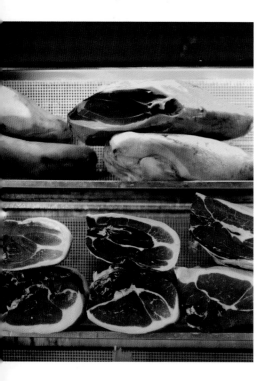

Carluccio

ZUPPA DI FAGIOLI CANNELLINI E COTENNE
Piedmontese Pork and Bean Soup

This mighty soup, also known as fagioli grassi _(fat beans), is almost a meal in itself. It is usually made in winter by the farmers when they kill the pig, and the bones are thrown into a bean stock to flavour it. In Ivrea every year, at the orange-throwing carnival held just before Lent, this soup is distributed gratis to the entire population. It is very much a_ cucina povera _dish and takes a while to cook, but the result is worth it._

Fill a large pan with the water and bring to the boil. Add the soup base ingredients, plus the pork ribs and skin. Return to the boil, lower the heat and leave to simmer for an hour.

Remove the pork skin pieces from of the soup, and flatten on a work surface, skin-side down. Divide the 'sausage' filling ingredients between the pieces, putting them in the middle of each piece. Season with salt and pepper and roll each up very tightly, like a sausage, with string.

Drain the soaked or canned beans. Put the pork skin 'sausages' back in the pan, along with the beans, and leave the soup to simmer for another hour, until the pork skin is very soft and gelatinous.

Scoop the fat from the top of the soup, and discard. Serve in deep bowls, accompanied by some good country bread.

2 litres **water**
900g **pork spare ribs**, cut into 8 pieces
4 x 15cm squares of **pork skin**, scraped free of fat, about 75g each
400g dried **cannellini beans**, soaked in water overnight, or 700g canned cannellini beans

SOUP BASE
2 tbsp **olive oil**
1 **onion**, halved
2 **celery stalks**, trimmed and finely chopped
1 large **carrot**, scrubbed and finely chopped
2 sprigs of **oregano** (or 1 tsp dried)
2 tbsp **tomato purée**

'SAUSAGE' FILLING
2 tbsp finely chopped **flat-leaf parsley**
1 **garlic clove**, finely puréed
1 tsp finely chopped **chilli**
½ tsp freshly grated **nutmeg**
1 tbsp dried **oregano**
salt and freshly ground **black pepper**

SERVES 4

400g **Savoy cabbage**, roughly
   sliced
500g piece **gammon**
1 large **onion**, roughly chopped
1 **celery stalk**, roughly chopped
   and a few leaves
1 large **carrot**, roughly chopped
1 **potato**, roughly chopped
8 **cherry tomatoes**
½ tsp **fennel seeds**
8 **peppercorns**
2 litres **water**
250g **batavia lettuce**
salt or powdered **vegetable stock**,
   to taste (optional)
extra virgin olive oil,
   for drizzling

SERVES 4

CONTALDO

MINESTRA MARITATA
Soup of Spring Greens and Pork

The English translation of this recipe's title is 'married soup' because the vegetables and meat marry so well together. It is a cucina povera *dish that traditionally featured on the Easter menu, as it uses up cheap cuts of pig which would have been preserved in salt since its slaughter in winter, as well as a combination of wonderful spring greens. Today, this soup is not served so much because of the large number of ingredients traditionally called for: a ham leg bone, salami, sausages, pork chops, pork rind; and for the vegetables, escarole, green cabbage, wild herbs such as fennel, dandelion and rocket. I really wanted to include it here though, so I have simplified the ingredients, but of course feel free to add any of the above if you so wish.*

Add the cabbage to a pan of boiling salted water and blanch for 5 minutes. Drain and set aside.

Place all the ingredients, except for the cabbage, lettuce, salt or stock and oil in a large saucepan and bring to the boil. Lower the heat, cover with a lid and leave to simmer gently for 1 hour.

Remove the gammon from the soup and chop into rough pieces, discarding any fat. Return to the soup, along with the lettuce and blanched cabbage. Check the seasoning, if necessary, add a little salt or powdered vegetable stock to taste. Cover with a lid and cook for a further 40 minutes, until the vegetables are tender. Remove from the heat and serve drizzled with olive oil and accompanied by some good country bread.

CONTALDO

400g **spaghetti**, linguine or
    tagliatelle
12 tbsp **extra virgin olive oil**
2 **garlic cloves**, finely chopped
½ **red chilli**, finely chopped
a handful of **basil leaves**, roughly
    torn
1 **beef tomato**, deseeded and
    cubed
1 **unwaxed lemon**, cut into small
    segments
grated zest and juice of 1 **lemon**
salt and freshly ground **black
    pepper**
40g **Parmesan**, freshly grated
20g **butter**

SERVES 4

PASTA AL LIMONE E BASILICO
Pasta with Lemon and Basil

*This quick pasta dish is easy to make. It is popular in southern Italy
in the warmer months, especially in Amalfi, where lemons grow in
abundance. The refreshing taste of lemon and the pungent aroma
of fresh basil marry well together.*

Bring a large saucepan of slightly salted water to the boil, add the pasta
and cook until *al dente*.

Meanwhile, heat the olive oil in a large frying pan, add the garlic and
chilli and sweat over a medium heat until soft, about a minute.

Drain the pasta, reserving a few tablespoons of the cooking water, and
add to the pan with the garlic and chilli and stir. Add a little of the
cooking water with the basil, tomato and lemon segments, zest and
juice. Season with a little salt and pepper. If the sauce is too thick, add
a little more cooking water. Stir in the Parmesan and butter, remove
from the heat and serve immediately.

300g Italian '00' flour
100g **semolina**
2 **eggs**

CONTALDO

PASTA FRESCA
Fresh Pasta

Making fresh pasta is not as difficult as you may think. At the restaurants I make it with an electric pasta machine, while at home I make it the traditional way by hand and with a small Imperia hand pasta machine. I recommend you purchase one of these as it will make life much easier – they are not very expensive and widely available these days. (I remember when I first came to England I had to bring my own from Italy!)

Mix the flour and semolina together on a clean work surface or in a large bowl. Make a well in the centre and break in the eggs. With a fork or with your hands, gradually mix the flour with the eggs until combined, then knead with your hands until you get a smooth, soft dough – it should be pliable but not sticky. Shape the dough into a ball, wrap in clingfilm and leave for about 30 minutes, or until you are ready to use.

Divide the pasta dough into four portions and put each one through your pasta machine, starting at the highest setting. Turn down the setting on the machine by one and repeat the process until you get to number 1 and your dough is almost wafer-thin.

Place the sheet of pasta onto a lightly floured work surface and use according to your recipe.

NON-EGG FRESH PASTA
For vegans or anyone who cannot eat eggs, simply substitute 120ml hot (but not boiling) water for the eggs and make as above.

PASTA CONTALDO
While pasta's exact origins are unknown, it is acknowledged that, by the 8th century, the Arabs had introduced it to Sicily. Nowadays there are endless varieties, and most Italians enjoy pasta at least once a day. As with all Italian food, pasta is very regional in its shapes, sauces and recipes. In the north, filled pastas such as *ravioli*, *cappelletti* and *tortellini* are common. In Rome, *bucatini all'amatriciana* and *spaghetti alla carbonara* are found on restaurant menus, while further south, you'll find richer slow-cooked *ragù*.

Baked pasta dishes like lasagne differ from north to south. The northern one, with its *ragù Bolognese* and béchamel sauce, is probably the best known abroad. In the south, we make a much richer version, replacing the *ragù* with meatballs, adding boiled eggs, salami, leftover vegetables, ricotta or mozzarella.

1 x **Fresh Pasta** recipe
  (see page 49), or 300g dried
  tagliatelle
125ml **white wine**
semolina, for dusting (optional)
freshly grated **Parmesan**
  (optional)

SAUCE
6 tbsp **extra virgin olive oil**
2 **garlic cloves**, finely chopped
1 small **red chilli**, finely chopped
  (optional)
400g mixed **wild mushrooms**,
  brushed, cleaned and roughly
  chopped
4 tbsp **white wine**
300ml **vegetable stock**
2 tbsp **flat-leaf parsley**, roughly
  chopped
salt

SERVES 4

CONTALDO

TAGLIATELLE AL VINO BIANCO CON FUNGHI
Fresh White Wine Pasta Ribbons with Mushrooms

This fresh pasta tagliatelle is made in the usual way, but with the addition of white wine, which makes it much lighter. In season, I urge you to use wild mushrooms, however the dish is just as delicious made with a mixture of cultivated mushrooms plus a few dried porcini (ceps), which you can find in most supermarkets.

Follow the recipe for fresh pasta (see page 49), pouring in the white wine when you add the beaten eggs to the flour.

To make tagliatelle, cut your pasta sheets into manageable sizes and run through the tagliatelle cutter on your machine. As the tagliatelle come out from the machine, gently roll into nests and lay on a flat tray sprinkled with some semolina. Alternatively, fold your pasta sheets into a loose roll and cut into ribbons of the desired width.

Heat the olive oil in a frying pan, add the garlic and chilli (if using) and sweat gently until softened. Raise the heat slightly, add the mushrooms and stir well for about a minute. Add the wine and allow to evaporate, then add the stock and cook, stirring, for a couple of minutes until the liquid has evaporated slightly. Stir in the parsley and season with salt to taste.

Meanwhile, bring a large pan of slightly salted water to the boil, add the tagliatelle and cook until *al dente* (fresh pasta will take only a couple of minutes, check the instructions on the packet for dried). Drain the pasta, reserving a little of the cooking water, and add to the mushroom mixture, stirring well. If the sauce is too thick, add a little of the cooking water. Remove from the heat and serve immediately with some freshly grated Parmesan, if desired.

CONTALDO

SPAGHETTI ALLA CRUDAIOLA
Spaghetti with Raw Tomatoes and Peppers

This is a simple pasta dish, perfect for easy entertaining, which is usually made in the summer in Italy using the season's best tomatoes. The sauce is raw – with the tomatoes left to marinate in good extra virgin olive oil – and can also be used to top crostini.

For the sauce, combine all the ingredients in a bowl, cover with a lid or foil and leave to marinate in the fridge for at least a couple of hours. You can leave the sauce overnight to develop a more intense flavour, but not longer.

When you are ready to use, remove the sauce from the fridge, check the seasoning, then set aside.

Bring a large saucepan of lightly salted water to the boil, add the spaghetti and cook until *al dente*. Drain the spaghetti, toss with the sauce and serve immediately, garnished with some basil leaves.

400g **spaghetti**
salt

SAUCE
240g **cherry tomatoes**, halved and deseeded
3 small sweet **green peppers**, finely sliced
1 tsp **capers**
1 small tender **celery stalk**, finely chopped
10 **basil leaves**, roughly torn, plus extra to garnish
a pinch of dried **oregano**
1 large **garlic clove**, finely chopped
125ml **extra virgin olive oil**

SERVES 4

350g *paccheri* pasta (available in good Italian delicatessens)

FILLING
3 tbsp **extra virgin olive oil**
1 large **onion**, finely chopped
3 **celery stalks**, roughly chopped
3 **carrots**, roughly chopped
1 tsp chopped **rosemary needles**
300g **courgette**, roughly chopped
50ml **white wine**
350g **passata**
2 tbsp **water**
salt and freshly ground **black pepper**

SAUCE
1 tbsp **extra virgin olive oil**
1 **garlic clove**, left whole
500g **asparagus**, roughly chopped
250ml **vegetable stock**
a pinch of **chilli powder** (optional)
50g grated **Parmesan**

SERVES 4

CONTALDO

PACCHERI RIPIENI CON SALSA D'ASPARAGI
Filled Pasta Tubes with Asparagus Sauce

Paccheri *are large hollow tubes and are either served with heavy ragù-type sauces, or filled as in this recipe. They are said to have been invented by Sicilian barons around the 1600s to smuggle garlic into Prussia after it banned the importation of (superior) Italian garlic. However, the Italians were not going to be beaten and up to five garlic cloves were smuggled inside each* pacchero, *eventually putting the Prussian garlic industry out of business!*

For the filling, heat the olive oil in a large frying pan, add the onion, celery, carrots and rosemary and sweat for about 3 minutes. Stir in the courgette, add the wine and allow to evaporate, then stir in the passata and water and season with salt and pepper. Cover with a lid and leave to simmer gently for about 30 minutes, until the sauce is thick and silky, stirring from time to time.

In the meantime, cook the *paccheri* in plenty of slightly salted water for 10 minutes. Drain well and leave to cool.

Preheat the oven to 180°C/Gas 4. For the sauce, heat the oil in a saucepan, add the garlic and leave to sweat for a couple of minutes. Discard the garlic and add the asparagus, stock and chilli powder, if using. Cook over a medium heat for 10 minutes. Remove from the heat and purée in a blender or food processor until smooth, then stir in half the Parmesan.

Lightly grease an ovenproof dish with some butter and spoon a little of the asparagus sauce onto the base. Place the *paccheri* upright in the dish, spoon in the vegetable filling and pour over the remaining sauce. Sprinkle with the remaining Parmesan and bake in the preheated oven for 25 minutes, until golden. Remove from the oven and leave to rest for a couple of minutes before serving.

TAGLIATELLE ALLA BOLOGNESE
Pasta Ribbons with Meat Sauce

Once and for all, spaghetti Bolognese *doesn't exist. If someone serves you this, they don't know anything about the cooking of Bologna, or they have run out of tagliatelle! There is a difference in what they call the 'mouth-feel' between tagliatelle and spaghetti, which feels entirely different on the palate. (It is better with fish sauces, plain tomato, or* carbonara, *in my opinion.) Meat sauces differ enormously in Bologna, and there is no one sauce which is most characteristic: some add livers or sweetbreads, or even milk. For me, this is the easiest and most traditional of all.*

To make the tagliatelle, cut your pasta sheets into manageable sizes and run through the tagliatelle cutter on your machine. As the tagliatelle come out from the machine, gently roll into nests and lay on a flat tray sprinkled with some semolina. Alternatively, fold your pasta sheets into a loose roll and cut into ribbons of the desired width.

For the sauce, fry the onion in the butter or oil until soft, about 5 minutes, then add the mince and brown, stirring to break up any large lumps. Add the wine and allow to evaporate, then stir in the tomato paste and tomato pulp, cover with a lid and heat until bubbling. Remove the lid and leave to simmer gently for 2 hours. If the sauce becomes too thick, you can add a little stock or water.

When the sauce is ready, cook the tagliatelle in plenty of boiling salted water until *al dente*, about 3–4 minutes if fresh (dried about 8–10). Drain and mix together with the sauce. Season to taste, sprinkle with the freshly grated Parmesan and serve immediately.

500g **Fresh Pasta** (see page 49), cut into tagliatelle, or 500g dried tagliatelle
semolina, for dusting (optional)
salt and freshly ground **black pepper**
80g **Parmesan**, freshly grated

SAUCE
1 large **white onion**, finely chopped
50g **butter** or 50ml extra virgin olive oil
500g mixed **pork and veal mince**, or veal and beef, or beef and pork (any combination you like)
100ml dry **white wine**
100g concentrated **tomato paste**
about 680g *polpa di pomodoro* or chunky passata

SERVES 6–8

1 x **Fresh Pasta** recipe
   (see page 49), or 300g dried
   tagliatelle
salt and freshly ground **black
   pepper**
2 tsp **truffle oil**
50–100g **Parmesan**, freshly
   grated
slices of **white truffle** (optional)

SAUCE
50g **unsalted butter**
1 small **onion**, cubed
400g **chicken livers**, cleaned and
   cut into small cubes
30g dried **porcini** (ceps), soaked
   for 20 minutes, then drained
   (reserving the water)
1 tbsp **tomato purée** (optional)
50ml **Marsala**, sherry or dry
   white wine

SERVES 4

TAJARIN CON FEGATINI
Thin Pasta Ribbons with Chicken Liver Sauce

Tajarin *is the Piedmontese dialect name for* tagliolini *or* tagliarini
*(thin ribbons of pasta). They are particularly connected with the
town of Alba – where this dish, with its sauce of chicken livers, is
also known as* tajarin all'albese *where a topping of the famous local
white truffle is added.* Tajarin *are served with many sauces, and
one famed for its simplicity is* sugo di arrosto, *the drippings left
over in the pan from a Sunday roast.*

Roll your fresh pasta into a very thin flat sheet and then into a loose
sausage shape. Cut across the sausage with a sharp knife to make thin
strands, about 3–4mm wide, and leave to rest on a bit of a clean cloth.

To make the sauce, melt the butter in a pan, add the onion and cook
for about 5–7 minutes, until it starts to turn golden. Add the chicken
livers, stir them around in the hot butter and fry for 3–4 minutes. Add
the drained porcini, tomato purée and Marsala, stir to combine and
season to taste. If the sauce appears too thick, add up to 4 tbsp of the
porcini-soaking water.

Meanwhile, cook the pasta in plenty of lightly salted boiling water
until *al dente*, then drain and mix with the sauce. Stir in the truffle oil
and sprinkle each serving with freshly grated Parmesan and the truffle
slices, if using.

Carluccio

TORTELLINI EMILIANI
Classic Tortellini with Meat Filling

It's odd that I chose to write this recipe, as the pasta shapes are very small, and with my big fingers, I find them quite difficult to make! (The answer, of course, is to make them bigger, as tortelloni.*) Also known as Venus's belly buttons, they are very fiddly, but delicious. The classic way of eating* tortellini *in Emilia-Romagna, where they hail from, is* in brodo *(in a good broth) as a pasta soup, but they are also good eaten with a simple tomato sauce or with sage, as here.*

Using a glass or something similar, cut your pasta sheets into little circles about 3–4cm in diameter. Cover with a damp cloth while you make the filling.

For the filling, boil the cabbage leaves in lightly salted water until very soft, about 15 minutes. Drain and leave to cool, then chop up roughly. In a blender, or with a hand blender, mince the cabbage, pork and *mortadella* together very finely, adding some salt, pepper and nutmeg to taste.

Put the pasta circles on a work surface. Put a little bit of the filling on one side of a circle, and fold the sides together over the filling to make a half-moon shape. Press to seal, using a little water to help them adhere. Then take the two outside edges and bring them together around your little finger, pressing together to seal. Cook in plenty of lightly salted boiling water for 1½ minutes, or until *al dente*.

Meanwhile, melt the butter in a pan, add the sage leaves and sauté for a minute or two. Add the Parmesan, and pour over the *tortellini*. Serve immediately.

1 x **Fresh Pasta** recipe
(see page 49)
salt and freshly ground **black pepper**
40g **unsalted butter**
8 **sage leaves**
50g **Parmesan**, freshly grated

FILLING
4 **Savoy cabbage leaves**
200g **roast pork**, roughly chopped
40g ***mortadella***, roughly chopped
freshly grated **nutmeg**

SERVES 4–6

THE NORTH-SOUTH DIVIDE

ITALY IS A HUGE COUNTRY, WITH TWENTY REGIONS WHICH DIFFER ENORMOUSLY IN TERMS OF CLIMATE, GEOGRAPHY, TOPOGRAPHY, LANGUAGE, CUSTOMS AND, OF COURSE, FOOD.
These regions were brought into existence when the country was united in 1861, but that didn't mean that there was a convergence of traditions and ideas. The historical and cultural differences were too great, and divisions persist between the regions even today. But a still deeper rift exists within the country itself, the cultural chasm between the north and south.

In brief, while the industrial north is wealthy, the agrarian south is comparatively poor, partly as a result of the neglect to which the area was subjected to various foreign occupiers throughout history, partly due to the more recent determination of politicians to industrialise the north, at the expense of the south. The differences in economic and social climates have led to general assumptions being made about the character of each area – broadly speaking, the north identifies itself with reason, forward thinking, sophistication, industriousness and progressiveness and considers the south to be lazy, superstitious and dependant on the north.

The south, known as the *mezzogiorno* (literally 'half' and 'day'), starts south of Rome and ends in Sicily. After World War II, in an attempt to develop the south, the Italian Government sent millions of dollars in aid, but monies were squandered and there was much scandal, corruption and organised crime. This wastefulness was the cause of much resentment and hostility in the north, and indeed led to the formation of a secessionist movement, Lega Nord, the 'Northern League', which tasked itself with promoting the future independence of northern Italy.

Everywhere you travel in Italy, you will encounter some reference to the north-south divide. The northerners disparagingly call the southerners *'terroni'* ('those of the land'), while southerners call the northerners *'polentoni'* (literally 'eaters of polenta'). Which brings us naturally to the north-south divide in food terms, for it certainly exists. Because of climate, the maize for polenta just happens to grow better in the north (as does rice). In fact, a better sobriquet for southerners might be 'maccheroni', because they famously eat so much pasta. When Garibaldi liberated Naples in 1861, he said 'It will be maccheroni, I swear to you, that will unite Italy'. That particular unity may not have been entirely achieved, but it is certainly true that both polenta and pasta, once foods of the poor, are now eaten everywhere.

Another major culinary divide is in the choice of cooking fat. Because the north is greener, and can support more animals, they use butter, whereas in the south, where olive trees flourish, the cooking medium is olive oil. As a result, the diet of the southerners is said to be much healthier, the famous 'Mediterranean diet'. And because the animal pastureland in the north is better, more meat is eaten, and made into various smallgoods (Parma ham, *cotechino* and *mortadella*, for example), while the milk from cows and sheep is made into cheeses such as Gorgonzola, Fontina, Parmesan and provolone, famous the world over. More fish and poultry are eaten in the south, and there are southern cheeses too (notably pecorino and mozzarella), but it is the vegetables, nuts and fruit – the tomatoes, aubergines, peppers, olives, artichokes, capers, almonds, oranges, lemons and limes – that are most characteristic of the area.

Things are changing, though, in the 'food' divide. During the 1950s and 1960s, many southerners made their way to the north for work, and there are sizeable numbers of *meridionali* (southerners) in the major northern cities. (Hence the arrival of lorry-loads of southern vegetables arriving each week in these cities.) The divide has also provided the world us with one large benefit – without it, the cooking of Italy would not be so well known elsewhere. Because the south was so economically depressed, millions of southerners had to seek work elsewhere, with many of the Italian restaurants and ice-cream parlours now found across the globe being a direct result of this southern Italian emigration. The ingredients that most characterise the cooking of Italy for the rest of the world are southern ingredients, popularised by those nostalgic for their homeland. Gennaro and I have done our bit too, of course!

Carluccio

CONTALDO

ORECCHIETTE CON BROCCOLI E ACCIUGHE
Ear-shaped Pasta with Broccoli and Anchovies

360g *orecchiette*
450g **broccoli florets**
6 tbsp **extra virgin olive oil**
2 **garlic cloves**, finely sliced
1 **red chilli**, finely sliced
6 **anchovy fillets**
salt

SERVES 4

*Orecchiette is the classic eggless pasta so traditional to Puglia.
This dish is eaten during all the region's saints' festivals, such as those
for Saint Nicolas and Saint Pio, and in fact all the restaurants around
the San Pio Monastery serve* orecchiette. *In Puglia it is made with*
cime di rapa, *which is widely grown there – as this type of broccoli is
not easily found here I have used broccoli florets, but you could also use
purple sprouting broccoli instead.*

Bring a large saucepan of slightly salted water to the boil, add the
orecchiette and cook for 3 minutes. Then add the broccoli and continue
to cook until the pasta is *al dente*.

Meanwhile, heat the olive oil in a large frying pan, add the garlic, chilli and
anchovies and stir-fry on a medium heat for a few minutes until the garlic
softens and the anchovies have almost dissolved into the oil. Drain the
pasta and broccoli, add to the pan, mix well and season with salt. Serve.

CONTALDO

PASTA CON FAGIOLI E COZZE
Pasta with Cannellini Beans and Mussels

This is a variation of the classic pasta e fagioli *(pasta and beans), with the addition of mussels. Dried cannellini beans are ideal but good-quality canned beans will suffice. If you are using dried beans, remember to soak them overnight and follow the cooking instructions on the packet. You can use pretty much any short pasta for this dish, or even a mixture if you want to finish up leftover packets in your cupboard.*

Clean the mussels by washing them under cold running water, scrubbing them well and pulling off the 'beards'. Leave to drain.

In a large pan, heat 2 tablespoons of olive oil and sweat the garlic for a minute until soft. Add the mussels and the wine, cover with a lid and cook on a high heat for about 5–6 minutes, shaking the pan occasionally, until the mussels have opened. Leave to cool a little, then remove the mussels from their shells (keeping a few for garnish) and strain, reserving the liquid. Discard any mussels that have not opened.

Heat the remaining oil in a pan, add the cannellini beans and sauté on a medium heat for 1 minute. Stir in the tomatoes, stock and the liquid from the mussels, bring to the boil, drop in the pasta and cook until *al dente*. Remove from the heat, stir in the mussels, sprinkle over the parsley and chilli and serve.

700g **mussels**
4 tbsp **extra virgin olive oil**, plus extra for drizzling
1 **garlic clove**, finely chopped
50ml **white wine**
450g **cannellini beans**, cooked and drained
200g tinned **chopped tomatoes**
100ml **vegetable stock**
200g **pasta**, such as *ditalini, gnocchetti sardi*, broken-up spaghetti, *fusilli* or *conchigliette*
a handful of **parsley**, finely chopped
½ **red chilli**, finely chopped

SERVES 4

400g **linguine**
salt and freshly ground **black**
  pepper

SAUCE
500g **mussels**
250g **prawns**
6 tbsp **olive oil**
1 **garlic clove**, crushed
½ **red chilli**, finely sliced
50ml **white wine**
juice of 1 **lemon**
a small bunch of **flat-leaf parsley**,
  roughly chopped

SERVES 4

Carluccio

LINGUINE CON COZZE E GAMBERETTI
Linguine with Mussels and Prawns

This is a regional dish par excellence, and perfect for a Friday night supper. Everywhere you go along the coastline of Italy it will be offered to you in some form or another, perhaps with cozze e vongole *(mussels and clams),* patelle *(limpets) and* moscardini *(baby octopus), scallops, squid, and/or a combination of all of them. The name of the dish may vary too, but basically it is* pasta ai frutti di mare *– seafood pasta.*

For the sauce, clean the mussels well, scrubbing them in cold water, and removing the beards. If any remain open after tapping them against the side of the work surface, discard them. Peel the prawns, removing the heads but leaving the tails intact.

Heat the olive oil in a large pan, and add the garlic and chilli. After a minute or two, add the mussels and the wine. Put the lid on and continue cooking until the mussels open, a few minutes only. If any remain closed at the end of cooking, discard them.

Add the prawns and cook for a further 4–5 minutes, turning them. Squeeze in the lemon juice. Take off the heat and add the roughly chopped parsley. Season to taste.

Meanwhile, cook the linguine in lightly salted boiling water until *al dente*, about 7–8 minutes. Add to the pan with the shellfish sauce, mix together well and serve immediately.

SEAFOOD CONTALDO

As the majority of Italy's regions are by the sea, it is no wonder there is such a variety of seafood available. From the Venice laguna in the north, to Sicily in the south, seaside restaurants sell an amazing array of dishes: fish stews, pasta sauces, preserved fish, fried fish, all of which differ slightly from region to region and village to village.

Italians are becoming more adventurous, though, and over the last 15 years Japanese-style sushi bars have opened up in Sardinia. Apparently the trend was started in a restaurant in Cagliari, using Sardinian tuna, and the idea spread throughout the island. When we returned to my home village of Minori to shoot part of the TV series, I went diving for octopus, and collected mussels and limpets from the rocks. That was a joyous time, transporting me back to the carefree days of my youth!

250g **plain flour**
a pinch of **salt**
400ml **water**
2 tbsp **extra virgin olive oil**, plus
    extra for oiling

SERVES 4

CONTALDO

TESTAROLI

This is an unusual type of primo, *traditionally made by the poor in the Lunigiana region, on the borders of Emilia-Romagna, Liguria and Tuscany, but which has now become something of a delicacy in local restaurants. The ingredients are very simply flour and water which are made into a batter. This is traditionally cooked in terracotta dishes locally known as* testetti, *which are placed on grills over an open fire. Obviously this method cannot easily be replicated at home, but a good-quality heavy-based pan is all you need to make this novel, pasta-like dish. Due to the filling nature of* testaroli, *a light sauce such as pesto or tomato (see opposite), is best.*

Sieve the flour and salt into a large bowl, gradually add the water and whisk well until you obtain a smooth batter. Whisk in the olive oil.

Lightly brush a large heavy-based frying pan with some oil and place over a high heat. When hot, add a ladleful of the batter to the pan and cook on each side for 3–4 minutes as you would a thick pancake. Remove, set aside and continue until you have used up all the batter.

With a sharp knife cut each of the *testaroli* into roughly 8 slices.

Bring a large saucepan of slightly salted water to the boil, drop in the testaroli and simmer until they rise to the top. Lift the *testaroli* out with a slotted spoon, drain well and serve immediately with your chosen sauce.

SALSA AL POMODORO CON GLI AROMI
Tomato Sauce with Herbs

This sauce traditionally goes with testaroli, but is just as delicious with pasta or gnocchi. SERVES 4

4 tbsp **extra virgin olive oil**
1 small **onion**, finely chopped
1 **garlic clove**, finely chopped
1 small **carrot**, finely chopped
a pinch of **oregano**
1 tbsp **parsley**, finely chopped
1 sprig of **thyme**
1 sprig of **rosemary**
400g tinned **plum tomatoes**, chopped
salt and freshly ground **black pepper**

Heat the oil in a pan, add the onion, garlic, carrot and herbs and stir-fry for a couple of minutes. Add the tomatoes, season with salt and pepper, cover with a lid and simmer gently for about 15 minutes.

PESTO
Fresh Basil Sauce

This sauce is from Liguria where lovely, sweet basil grows in abundance. Fresh pesto keeps in the fridge for about a week but you can also make batches and freeze them for later use. If you keep it in the fridge, make sure you pour some extra virgin oil over the top to preserve it. SERVES 4

2 tbsp **pine kernels**
1 **garlic clove**
½ tsp **salt**
80g **basil leaves**, stalks removed
200ml **extra virgin olive oil**
2 tbsp freshly grated **pecorino** or Parmesan

Place the pine kernels, garlic and salt in a mortar and grind to a paste with a pestle. Add a few basil leaves and some of the olive oil and grind and stir with the pestle. Continue like this until you have used up all the basil leaves and about half the olive oil and the sauce has a silky consistency. Finally, add the remaining olive oil and the cheese and mix well.

PIZZA
190g **quick-cook polenta**
2 tbsp **olive oil**
salt and freshly ground **black
pepper**
about 220ml boiling **water**

MENESTA
6 **garlic cloves**, chopped
1 fresh **red chilli**, finely chopped
4 tbsp **olive oil**
500g **wild chicory**, or other
greens such as broccoli, sea
kale, spinach or dandelions,
prepared as necessary
50ml **water**

SERVES 4

POLENTA CONTALDO

Before the introduction of maize from
the Americas, the Italian porridge,
polenta, was made with varying
ingredients, including chestnuts. At first
maize was used for animal feed, until
peasants discovered it could be ground
into flour to make polenta as well as
bread and cakes. Up until the mid 1900s,
this maize-flour meal would be the
only thing peasants ate: it is said while
southern Italian farmers worked in the
fields with their bellies full of pasta, so
northern Italians subsisted on little more
than polenta for centuries!

Polenta is still very popular today both
at home and on restaurant menus. It can
be served 'wet', by itself, with cheese and
other flavourings (see page 121), or as the
perfect accompaniment to a good *ragù*. It
can also be left to 'set', after which cut-out
shapes can be grilled, baked or fried to be
served with fish, meat or vegetables.

Carluccio

PIZZA E MENESTA
Braised Greens with Polenta Cake

This cucina povera *dish is found in the area around Naples,
but it is different from the normal pizza, in that it is made with
cornmeal or polenta.* Pizza or pitta *means something flat (a cake,
for instance), and* menesta *is the Neapolitan for* minestra, *a soupy
braise of vegetables. If you can't find wild chicory (my green of
choice), the Belgian kind will do, or you could use purple sprouting
broccoli (pictured), sea kale, spinach, even dandelions. Mushrooms
are good too, surprisingly. The braised greens should have a slightly
bitter flavour. If using Belgian chicory, add 4–5 small tomatoes,
halved, and a tablespoon of capers, for extra flavour.*

To make the *menesta*, put the garlic, chilli and half the olive oil
into a medium pan and heat gently. When the garlic starts to colour,
add the greens and water. Put the lid on and cook until soft, about
10–15 minutes.

Meanwhile, for the *pizza*, put the polenta in a bowl with half the olive
oil and season. Pour in the boiling water and stir to make a crumbly
but pliable dough. Leave to cool a little, then divide into four pieces.
Shape each into flat hamburger-like shapes, about 2.5cm thick and
5cm in diameter.

Pour the remaining olive oil into a large frying pan and heat gently.
Add the cakes and cook for about 5–6 minutes on each side, until a
thick crust has formed and the edges are slightly burned.

Arrange the polenta and the greens on plates, spooning a couple of
tablespoons of the cooking juices from the greens over each plate.

500ml **milk**
500ml **water**
salt and freshly ground **black pepper**
250g **semolina** flour
4 **egg yolks**
freshly grated **nutmeg**
olive oil, for oiling
100g **unsalted butter**
50g **Parmesan**, freshly grated

SERVES 8–10

Carluccio

GNOCCHI ALLA ROMANA
Semolina Dumplings Roman Style

This kind of gnocchi is completely different to other gnocchi, being made of semolina rather than flour and potato, spinach or pumpkin. A speciality of Rome – and popular throughout the entire province – they are delicious, flavoured with nutmeg, Parmesan and black pepper. They are also very filling, so serve in small portions.

Preheat the oven to 180°C/Gas 4.

Put the milk and water in a large saucepan with a little salt, and bring to the boil. Add the semolina flour and cook gently, whisking constantly, until the mixture is semi-solid, about 2 minutes. Take off the heat and allow to cool slightly.

Fold the egg yolks into the warm semolina, add a pinch of freshly grated nutmeg and season with salt and pepper. Spread on an oiled cool marble or metal surface and flatten to a 1cm thickness. Leave to cool and set, then cut out rounds, using a 4–5cm cutter or glass. (The leftovers can be baked with tomatoes and mozzarella, as a snack. In Italy nothing is thrown away!)

Grease an ovenproof dish and lay the semolina rounds, overlapping, in it. Dot with the rest of the butter, season with salt and pepper and sprinkle over the Parmesan and another pinch of freshly grated nutmeg. Bake for about 10 minutes.

Serve as they are, or with a little tomato sauce (see page 69) spooned over the top.

1kg floury **potatoes**, roughly the
  same size
salt and freshly ground **black
  pepper**
1 **egg**
300g **plain flour**
rice flour, for dusting

SAUCE
5 tbsp **extra virgin olive oil**
1 **garlic clove**
700g tinned **chopped tomatoes**
a handful of **basil**, roughly torn,
  plus a few extra whole leaves to
  garnish
200g **mozzarella**
100g **Parmesan**, freshly grated

SERVES 4–6

CONTALDO

GNOCCHI ALLA SORRENTINA
Potato Gnocchi with Tomato and Mozzarella

*I urge you to try making your own gnocchi, they really are delicious!
If, however, you find yourself pressed for time, you can substitute
an 800g packet of prepared potato gnocchi instead. This simple
tomato sauce, with the addition of mozzarella cheese, is typical of
Campania, which produces the best tomatoes and mozzarella.*

Place the unpeeled potatoes in a saucepan and cover with cold water.
Bring to the boil, lower the heat and simmer until the potatoes are
tender, but not falling apart. Drain, allow to cool a little and remove
the skins. Mash and leave to cool.

Place the cooled mashed potato in a large bowl, season with salt, stir in
the egg, add the flour and work to obtain a smooth but sticky dough.
On a clean work surface, sprinkle the rice flour and roll out the dough
into long sausage shapes. With a sharp knife slice into 2cm squares.
Set aside.

To make the sauce, heat the olive oil in a large frying pan, add the
garlic and sweat for a minute until soft. Add the tomato and torn basil,
season with salt and pepper and bring to the boil. Lower the heat, half
cover with a lid and simmer for 10 minutes.

Bring a large saucepan of slightly salted water to the boil. Drop the
gnocchi into the water and simmer until they rise to the top. Lift them
out with a slotted spoon, drain well and add to the tomato sauce. Stir
in the mozzarella and half of the Parmesan and cook for a further
minute or so, until the mozzarella begins to melt. Remove from the
heat, sprinkle over the remaining Parmesan, garnish with the basil
leaves and serve immediately.

NDUNDARI CON SALSA DI POMODORO E BASILICO
Ricotta Dumplings with Tomato and Basil Sauce

This is one of my favourite recipes from home and I just had to put it in this book. These little dumplings, made from a few staple Italian larder ingredients, are traditionally made in my home village of Minori on the feast day of the town's patron saint. When I return to Minori, it pleases me to see this now on the menus of the best restaurants, so that not only locals but also tourists can enjoy this simple, but truly delicious dish.

In a large bowl, mix the flour, ricotta, egg yolks, Parmesan, nutmeg and a pinch of salt and pepper together to form a soft, moist dough. Place on a floured work surface and knead for 3–5 minutes. With your hands, roll the dough into a long, thin sausage shape and then cut it at right angles into rectangular shapes about 2cm long.

Bring a large saucepan of lightly salted water to the boil and add the dumplings. Wait until they rise to the surface again, then lower the heat and simmer for a further 2 minutes.

Meanwhile, make the sauce. Place the tomatoes and basil in a bowl, season with salt and pepper and mix well. Heat the olive oil in a large pan and add the garlic. When the garlic begins to change colour, remove the pan from the heat and add the tomato mixture. Replace on the heat and cook gently for 4 minutes, until the mixture is bubbling.

Drain the dumplings with a slotted spoon and add to the tomato sauce. Mix thoroughly and serve immediately.

200g Italian **'00' flour,** plus extra for flouring
220g **ricotta**
3 **egg yolks**
20g **Parmesan,** freshly grated
a pinch of freshly grated **nutmeg**
salt and freshly ground **black pepper**

SAUCE
700g tinned **plum tomatoes**, chopped in half
a few **basil leaves**
6 tbsp **olive oil**
3 **garlic cloves**, cut into thick slices

SERVES 4

CONTALDO

RISOTTO CON PECORINO, OLIO E ACETO BALSAMICO
Risotto with Pecorino, Olive Oil and Balsamic Vinegar

A plain risotto with some butter or olive oil and cheese is great comfort food as well as being quick to make. I made this risotto when I had nothing in the house but a chunk of Sardinian pecorino cheese, some risotto rice and extra virgin olive oil. When it was ready, I livened it up a little with a few drops of aged balsamic vinegar, and I was really pleased with my 'fast-food' meal. It is amazing how a few good regional ingredients can come together to create such a sophisticated dish.

Put the stock in a saucepan and bring to a gentle simmer. Leave over a low heat.

Heat 2 tablespoons of the olive oil in a medium-sized saucepan and sweat the onion until soft. Add the rice and stir until all the grains are coated with oil, then add the white wine and keep stirring until it evaporates. Add a couple of ladlefuls of the stock and cook, stirring all the time, until it has been absorbed. Repeat with more stock. Continue adding the stock in this way until the rice is cooked *al dente*, which usually takes about 20 minutes. Check for seasoning and adjust if necessary.

Remove from the heat and beat in the pecorino and the remaining olive oil with a wooden spoon. Leave to rest for a minute, then divide between four plates. Drizzle with some balsamic vinegar, sprinkle with some more pecorino and serve.

1.5 litres **vegetable stock**
4 tbsp **extra virgin olive oil**
½ small **onion**, very finely chopped
350g **arborio risotto rice**
50ml **white wine**
80g **pecorino**, freshly grated, plus extra to serve
balsamic vinegar, for drizzling

SERVES 4

OLIVE OIL CONTALDO

Italy is one of the world's top producers of olive oil and extra virgin olive oil, and the country's different varieties of olives, differing growing conditions, harvest times and number of pressings combine to create a diversity of flavours throughout the Italian regions. In Liguria the small Taggiasca olives produce a light, delicate oil; Tuscany's more peppery-tasting oil comes from Frantoio, Puntino, Maurino and Leccino olives, while further south in Puglia and Sicily, the olive oil becomes stronger, sharper and more fruity in taste.

Olive oil is big business in Italy and in the early 1990s the DOP (*Denominazione di Origine Protetta*) certification was introduced for producers. If a bottle of olive oil has this mark, it means that the oil has been put through a very particular and scrupulous quality control process in its area of origin.

2 litres **chicken stock**
(see page 38)
1 **garlic clove**, finely chopped
2 **celery stalks**, trimmed and
finely chopped
1 **carrot**, scraped and finely
chopped
1 **onion**, peeled and finely
chopped
50g **unsalted butter**
5 tbsp **olive oil**
240g **carnaroli risotto rice**
2 small **courgettes**, finely
chopped
salt and freshly ground **black
pepper**
50g **Parmesan**, freshly grated,
plus extra to serve
5 **courgette flowers**

SERVES 4

RISOTTO CON FIORI DI ZUCCHINI
Risotto with Courgette Flowers

*One of the most delicate, pretty and tasty dishes you can prepare
in early summer is a risotto made with courgettes and their
flowers. Courgettes have two sort of flowers, those attached to small
courgettes (which are female) and those simply attached to a stalk
(male). Both can be used, and although expensive to buy (even in
Italy), if you have a garden, or a friend who grows courgettes, you
can have them for nothing! The flowers don't taste of much, but
there is a wonderful delicacy about their texture – and stuffed and
fried as an antipasto they are delicious.*

Have the stock in a pan beside where you will cook the risotto, and
heat it to a simmer.

Put the garlic, celery, carrot and onion in a large pan with half the
butter and all the olive oil, and sweat until soft, about 7 minutes. Add
the rice and stir for a minute, then start to add the hot stock, a couple
of ladlefuls at first, and stir until you see that the rice has absorbed the
liquid. Add a little more stock, and stir until that has been absorbed as
well. Continue adding liquid in the same way. After 10 minutes stirring
and cooking, add the courgette pieces. Continue to cook the same
way until the rice is *al dente*, making sure the last addition of stock is
enough to keep the rice loose but not wet.

Add salt and pepper to taste, and beat in the remaining butter and
the Parmesan. Fold in the courgette flowers and serve immediately,
sprinkled with Parmesan.

RICE, PASTA AND GRAINS
CONTALDO

Rice, pulses and grains are staples around
the world. The most important grain in
Italy, wheat, is used to make bread and
pasta, and the introduced maize is the
basis of the northern polenta. Rice was
introduced to the Po Valley in northern
Italy by the Arabs during the 14th
century and is now a northern staple,
and the basis of the famous risotto.

Couscous, made from semolina
wheat, is eaten in Sicily (introduced
to the island by the Arabs) and is now
appearing in mainland Italy due to
North African immigration, while lesser-
known but highly nutritious grains
such as buckwheat, barley and spelt are
gradually becoming more popular.

CONTALDO

RISOTTO ALLA MARINARA CON VERDURE
Seafood and Vegetable Risotto

1 litre **vegetable stock**
600g **mussels**
600g **clams**
7 tbsp **extra virgin olive oil**
1 **garlic clove**, left whole
150g **baby squid**, sliced
150g **prawns**
1 small **onion**, finely chopped
1 small **carrot**, finely chopped
400g **arborio risotto rice**
50ml **white wine**
200g **courgettes**, finely chopped
200g **red pepper**, finely chopped
salt and freshly ground **black pepper**
a handful of **parsley**, finely chopped

SERVES 4–6

I dedicate this recipe to the Giardiniello Restaurant in my home village of Minori, which has been making this beautiful dish since it opened in 1955. When I make it, I'm reminded of those summer evenings when, as a little boy, my mother would take me to enjoy a late-night supper cooked by Nunziatina, the owner and chef.

Bring the stock to the boil in a saucepan and keep it at a low simmer.

Clean the mussels and clams by washing them in plenty of cold water, scrubbing them well and removing any beards. Heat 3 tablespoons of the oil in a large pan, add the garlic and sweat for a minute, then add the mussels and clams. Cook, covered, on a high heat for a few minutes, until the shells open. Remove from the heat and leave to cool, discarding any unopened shells. Extract the flesh from the shells, (retaining a few for garnish) and strain and set aside the cooking liquid.

Meanwhile, heat 2 tablespoons of olive oil in another pan, add the baby squid and stir-fry for 4 minutes, then add the prawns, mussels and clams with the cooking liquid and cook for a further minute in order for the flavours to infuse. Remove from the heat and set aside.

In a medium-sized saucepan, heat the remaining oil, add the onion and carrot and sweat. Add the rice and stir for a minute. Pour in the wine and keep stirring until it evaporates, then start to add the hot stock, ladle by ladle, waiting until each ladleful has been absorbed before you add the next. After 10 minutes' cooking and stirring, add the courgettes, red pepper, seafood and cooking liquid and season to taste. Continue to cook and add stock in the same way until the rice is *al dente*. Remove from the heat, stir in half the parsley and leave to rest for a minute before serving with the reserved shells and the remaining parsley.

1.5 litres **fish stock**
600g **cuttlefish**, preferably small
6 tbsp **olive oil**
1 **onion**, very finely chopped
300g **vialone nano rice**
50ml **dry white wine**
salt and freshly ground **black pepper**
50g **unsalted butter**, cut into cubes (optional)

SERVES 6

Carluccio

RISOTTO CON SEPPIE
Risotto with Cuttlefish

This must be the signature dish of Venice, a risotto coloured black by the ink of cuttlefish caught in the Laguna. Originally it would have been a fisherman's dish, but now it can be found in almost every restaurant in the city. The cuttlefish of the Venetian laguna are slightly different from those of elsewhere, being smaller, bright in colour when alive and full of ink. If you buy your cuttlefish from the supermarket they may already been cleaned and had the ink sacs removed, in which case you will need to buy a few sachets of ink to colour the rice.

Bring the stock to the boil in a pan and keep it at a low simmer.

Clean the little cuttlefish very thoroughly, removing the striped skin, beak, eyes innards and bone and retaining the bodies, tentacles and the silver-coloured ink sacs (which will need to be carefully detached). Squeeze the ink from the sacs into a small saucer and chop the cuttlefish bodies into pieces.

Heat the oil in a large pan, add the onion and cook until brown, about 7 minutes. Add the cuttlefish and tentacles, then the rice, stirring to coat it with fat. Pour in the wine and keep stirring until it evaporates, then start to add the hot stock, ladle by ladle, waiting until each ladleful has been absorbed before you add the next. After 10 minutes cooking and stirring, add the cuttlefish ink and continue to cook until the rice is *al dente*. Season with salt and pepper to taste and beat in the butter, if using. (This will make the risotto smooth and shiny and is a process called *mantecare*, or *manteca* in Venice). Leave to rest for a few minutes before serving.

Carluccio

2 litres **chicken or beef stock** (see page 38)
4 tbsp **olive oil**
100g **unsalted butter**
1 **onion**, finely chopped
280g **carnaroli** or **vialone nano risotto rice**
2 sachets **powdered saffron**, or 1g saffron strands
50g **Parmesan**, freshly grated
salt and freshly ground **black pepper**

SERVES 4

RISOTTO MILANESE
Saffron Risotto

This is the classic risotto to accompany Osso Buco in Bianco *(see page 129) and its unique colour and flavour depends on the use of saffron, the highly expensive spice which was once one of the main commodities traded by the Doges of Venice. I prefer to use good quality powdered saffron rather than saffron strands, as it dissolves more easily, but if you do use strands, you can make them easier to dissolve by toasting them in a metal spoon over a gas flame. When they have cooled a little, they can be crumbled to a virtual powder.*

Put the stock in a saucepan and bring to a gentle simmer. Leave over a low heat.

Heat the oil in a large pan with half the butter and fry the onion until soft, about 7 minutes. Add the rice and stir for a minute, then start to add the hot stock, ladle by ladle. Avoid drowning the rice in stock, and wait until each ladleful is absorbed before you add the next. After 10 minutes cooking and stirring, add the powdered saffron. Continue to cook and add stock in the same way until the rice is *al dente*, then add the rest of the butter and the grated Parmesan and season with salt and pepper to taste.

Serve either on its own or as an accompaniment to *Osso Buco in Bianco* (see page 129).

SECONDI
MAIN COURSES

WHEN YOU HAVE EATEN A *PRIMO* (AND PERHAPS EVEN SEVERAL ANTIPASTI) THEN YOU ARE READY TO TACKLE THE *SECONDI*, OR MAIN COURSE, which traditionally consists of meat or fish served with a *contorno* (side dish of vegetables or salad). None of these are usually large, perhaps primarily because the Italians like to accompany almost everything with bread. With *secondi* this is usually a substantial country bread or ciabatta, with which to mop up the sauce!

Carluccio
Italians love to hunt, and nothing is sacred. In certain areas they shoot or catch and eat sparrows as well as thrushes, blackbirds and ortolan. Wild goat and boar, venison and marmot (squirrel) are shot. The hunting season is very short, and millions of Italians take part, often perforating their own backsides with pellets!

Italians eat anything that moves on two or four legs and meat can be anything from a simple quick-fry steak to more elaborate pot roasts, boiled meats or stews. Veal is very popular and much loved for its white delicate flesh. Lamb and kid are also eaten, as is offal in all its forms – a tradition from the days when no food was wasted and the Italian housewife had to make use of all parts of the animal. These dishes have become specialities, and very much form part of the Italian diet.

The majority of Italian regions have access to the sea, so fish forms a major part of the diet – and even in areas with no coastline, there are freshwater fish to be enjoyed and, of course, the beloved *baccalà* (salted air-dried cod). Dishes and methods of cooking differ from region to region, as do the fish themselves: swordfish and tuna are typical of Calabria and Sicily, sardines and anchovies of Sardinia, while the Adriatic coast boasts a multitude of fish and seafood with which to prepare different *brodetti* (fish soups), sauces for pasta, or to serve simply grilled, poached, baked or steamed with olive oil and lemon.

Vegetables are also served as *secondi*, and there are many delicious vegetarian main courses. Aubergines and courgettes can be layered with cheese as *parmigiane*, or they can be filled and baked. Onions, artichokes, tomatoes, peppers and, a seasonal treat, courgette flowers, can also be filled and cooked. Many vegetables are included in tarts or *calzoni* (folded pizzas), or *frittate* (omelettes). Beans and pulses too form a very important part of the Italian diet and ways of cooking them vary, as in everything, from region to region.

CONTALDO

ZUCCHINI ALLA PARMIGIANA
Courgette and Cheese Bake

This is an alternative to the traditional aubergine version, which is so popular throughout Italy, the courgettes making it lighter and fresher tasting. You can eat it hot or cold, and it makes a wonderful vegetarian main course served with a mixed salad.

To make the tomato sauce, heat the olive oil in a saucepan, add the onion and sweat until softened. Add the tomatoes, torn basil and salt, then cover the pan and simmer gently for about 15 minutes.

Preheat the oven to 200°C/Gas 6. Dust the courgette slices in flour, then dip them in the beaten egg.

Pour enough vegetable oil into a frying pan to cover the base generously and heat gently. Add the courgette slices and fry on both sides until golden. Remove and drain on kitchen paper.

Line a 20 x 22cm ovenproof dish with some of the tomato sauce, then arrange a layer of courgettes followed by another layer of tomato sauce and some of the mozzarella, Parmesan and basil leaves. Continue layering in this way until you use up all the ingredients, making sure to end up with a topping of cheese.

Cover with foil and bake in the oven for 20 minutes. Remove the foil and continue to bake for a further 20 minutes, until the top is golden. Remove from the oven and leave to to rest for 5 minutes before serving.

3 large **courgettes**, cut lengthways into slices about 5mm thick
plain flour, for dusting
4 **eggs**, lightly beaten with some salt and pepper
vegetable oil
200g **hard mozzarella**, cubed
5 tbsp freshly grated **Parmesan**
a few **basil leaves**

SAUCE
2 tbsp **extra virgin olive oil**
1 small **onion**, finely chopped
500g tinned **plum tomatoes**
a few **basil leaves**, roughly torn
a pinch of **salt**

SERVES 4

6 **eggs**
75g **Parmesan**, freshly grated
a bunch of **basil leaves**, roughly
   torn, reserving a few whole
   leaves to garnish
salt and freshly ground **black
   pepper**
2 tbsp **extra virgin olive oil**

SERVES 2

CONTALDO

FRITTATA AL BASILICO
Basil Omelette

In these busy times, what could be simpler to cook after a hectic day's work and commute than an omelette? It is also an ideal meal if your cupboard is bare: most people will have eggs, Parmesan or other cheese in the fridge, and certainly for Italians it is not uncommon to keep a basil plant or two on the balcony. A frittata is quite a popular main course to have in Italy, especially for the evening meal: it is quick, easy, economical and nutritious.

Beat the eggs in a bowl together with the Parmesan and the torn basil leaves. Season with salt and pepper.

Heat the olive oil in a frying pan over a medium heat, pour the egg mixture into the pan and cook until the bottom is golden, about 5 minutes. Turn the omelette over and cook until the other side turns golden-brown, about 3 minutes. Remove from the heat, cut in half and serve hot or cold, garnished with a few basil leaves and accompanied by a simple green salad.

BASIL AND OTHER HERBS
CONTALDO

Herbs are widely used in Italian cooking. Basil is probably the most common; loved by Italians, it can be seen growing on balconies and in window boxes and the sweet variety used in dishes such as the classic Ligurian pesto.

I love picking oregano fresh and leaving it to dry; its pungency marries well with tomatoes and potatoes, and it's a must in *pizzaiola* sauce. Rosemary and sage are often used to flavour roast meats, and the northern combination of melted butter and sage leaves for dressing tortellini is hard to beat. Flat-leaf parsley is a great favourite in soups, stews, stocks and sauces, and with fish (in Italy fishmongers often give away bunches of it when you buy from them), while thyme, marjoram, mint and fennel are also used; their distinct, delicate flavours enhancing a wide variety of foods.

2 tbsp **olive oil**
500g fresh **porcini** (ceps), sliced,
  or 500g button mushrooms,
  plus 25g dried porcini (ceps),
  soaked for 30 minutes, then
  drained and finely sliced
salt and freshly ground **black
  pepper**
500ml **vegetable or chicken stock**
  (see page 38), or use a stock
  cube and boiling water
2 big discs *pane carasau*
unsalted butter, for greasing
150g **Fontina cheese**, or other
  melting cheese such as Taleggio
50g **Parmesan**, freshly grated

SAUCE
75g **unsalted butter**
100g **plain flour**
1 litre **full-fat milk**
a pinch of **nutmeg**

SERVES 8

Carluccio

LASAGNETTA CON PANE CARASAU
Sardinian Bread Lasagne

A lasagne is a baked dish, traditional served in Italy as part of a celebratory meal. It is usually made with sheets of pasta, but here I have used the crisp flatbread of Sardinia, known as pane carasau *or* carta di musica *('music sheet', so called because the bread is so thin you can read a sheet of music through it). So, this is not a traditional recipe but rather an exploration of an old idea that would make a great Christmas dish for vegetarians.*

Preheat the oven to 180°C/Gas 4. Heat the olive oil in a frying pan over a medium heat, add the mushrooms and fry for about 3 minutes, sprinkling with a little salt. Drain on kitchen paper and set aside.

Put the stock into a flat container or oven tray large enough to fit the *pane carasau*. Soak each disc of the crisp bread carefully in the stock for about 15 seconds on each side. Set the bread aside and pour the stock out of the tray (this can be used for a soup or another sauce). Wash, dry and then grease the tray lightly, before laying a piece of soaked *pane carasau* on its base.

To make the sauce, melt the butter in a saucepan, stir in the flour and cook for 1 minute, then add the milk gradually, stirring all the time, until smooth. Add the nutmeg, season to taste and set aside.

Spread half of the sauce over the first layer of soaked bread in the oven tray. Arrange the mushrooms evenly all over, reserving a few. Sprinkle the mushrooms with the grated Fontina, and place the second piece of soaked bread on top of this. Pour over the remaining sauce, scatter over the remaining mushroom slices, sprinkle generously with pepper, and then sprinkle over the Parmesan. Bake in the preheated oven for 15 minutes, until golden-brown. Cut into wedges to serve.

CONTALDO

vegetable oil, for frying
3 aubergines, cut into small
  cubes
3 tbsp freshly grated Parmesan
1 egg
salt and freshly ground black
  pepper
6 basil leaves, roughly torn
60g stale bread, softened in water
dried breadcrumbs (see page
  154), for coating

MAKES 14 POLPETTE

POLPETTE DI MELANZANE
Aubergine Dumplings

*Aubergines have quite a meaty texture and make a lovely
vegetarian alternative to meatballs. These dumplings used to be
made when meat was scarce or could not be eaten during religious
times such as Lent. Served with a freshly made tomato sauce (such
as the* Salsa Al Pomodoro Con Gli Aromi *on page 69), they are
so tasty that once I have one I can't stop! For a healthier version,
rather than cubing and frying the aubergines, try halving them,
making incisions all over the flesh with a knife and roasting them
in a hot oven at 220°C/Gas 7 for about 20 minutes, until the
aubergine pulp is soft. Leave to cool, then scoop the flesh out and
combine with the rest of the ingredients as below.*

Pour enough vegetable oil into a large frying pan to cover the base
generously, add the aubergine cubes and stir-fry until golden-brown.
Remove from the pan, drain well on kitchen paper and leave to cool.

In a bowl, combine the aubergines, Parmesan, egg, some salt and
pepper, basil and bread. Roll the mixture into walnut-sized balls and
coat in breadcrumbs.

Replace the vegetable oil in the frying pan with new oil and heat
gently. Add the aubergine balls and cook until golden-brown. Serve
immediately, with *Salsa Al Pomodoro Con Gli Aromi* (see page 69).

CONTALDO

PANE COTTO
Bread and Potatoes

1.3 litres **vegetable stock**
600g **potatoes**, peeled and cut
    into walnut-sized chunks
240g stale **country bread**, cut
    into 6cm pieces
4 tbsp **extra virgin olive oil**
4 slices **pancetta** or bacon
1 small **red chilli**

SERVES 4

This is a typical cucina povera *recipe. Traditionally the potatoes would probably not have been cooked in any stock and pancetta was certainly not used, but perhaps a little melted lard and crushed chilli would have been added to give some extra flavour. Despite its impoverished ingredients, this dish is really very tasty and makes an excellent quick meal if you have little in your cupboard.*

Bring the vegetable stock to the boil in a large saucepan. Add the potatoes and simmer until tender. Once the potatoes are cooked, remove from the pan and drop the bread pieces briefly into the stock, pressing down gently with a fork to ensure they have absorbed the liquid evenly. Drain and arrange with the potatoes on a plate.

Meanwhile, heat the olive oil in a frying pan, add the pancetta and chilli and stir-fry until the pancetta is golden and crispy. Spoon over the bread and potatoes and serve.

60g **sun-dried tomatoes**
40g **black olives**
100g **stale bread**
1 tbsp finely chopped **parsley**
salt and freshly ground **black pepper**
4 **cod fillets**, about 200g each
2 tbsp **extra virgin olive oil**
1 tbsp **white wine**

SERVES 4

CONTALDO

MERLUZZO IN CROSTA
Cod with an Olive and Sun-dried Tomato Crust

This is quite a modern way of cooking fish in Italy. Instead of serving a plain white fish – cod or hake – in the usual way with olive oil and lemon, a topping is made by combining finely chopped olives, sun-dried tomatoes and parsley. The ingredients of this simple to prepare crust are very southern Italian, and go extremely well with the fish.

Preheat the oven to 150°C/Gas 2.

Place the sun-dried tomatoes, olives, bread and parsley in a food processor and whiz until the mixture resembles breadcrumbs. (Alternatively, you could finely chop everything with a good, sharp knife.) Season with salt and pepper to taste and set aside.

Sprinkle a little salt over the cod fillets and place in a large ovenproof dish. Pour over the olive oil and white wine and bake in the oven for 5 minutes. Top with the breadcrumb mixture, return to the oven and cook for a further 10 minutes, until the breadcrumbs are golden and the fish has cooked through.

Serve immediately with some steamed green beans.

4 **red mullet**, about 300g each,
  gutted, trimmed and scaled
6 tbsp **olive oil**
2 **shallots**, finely chopped
1 **garlic clove**, finely chopped
700g *polpa di pomodoro*
  or chunky passata
6 **basil leaves**
salt and freshly ground **black
  pepper**
1 **lemon**, cut into quarters

SERVES 4

TRIGLIE ALLA LIVORNESE
Red Mullet with Tomatoes

Livorno, a town on the Tuscan Tyrrhenian coast, is well known for its fish dishes. The most famous is the cacciucco, *a fish stew (in which they are said to use as many fish varieties as there are c's in the name!). Anything labelled* alla livornese *means fish cooked with tomatoes, and this red mullet version is much loved locally.*

This delicate, simple dish also lends itself very well to being served with pasta. Simply bone and fillet the fish before cooking as below and serving with linguine.

In a frying pan large enough to hold all four fish, heat the oil. Add the shallots and garlic, and sauté gently until cooked but not coloured, about 5 minutes. Add the tomato pulp, basil and some salt and pepper to taste, then bring to the boil.

Reduce the heat to medium, add the fish and cook for about 6 minutes on each side

Serve the fish whole on individual plates with the lemon quarters and topped with some of the intensely flavoured sauce. Good bread is all that you need by way of accompaniment.

TOMATOES CONTALDO
Native to South America, tomatoes didn't appear in Italy until the 1500s, when Christopher Columbus returned to Europe. At first they were considered poisonous, and were not used in cooking until about the 18th century. Since then they quickly spread around the whole of the Mediterranean – where the climate was ideal – growing particularly well in the fertile lands between Naples and Salerno, which is where the famous San Marzano tomato comes from.

It would be hard to imagine Italian cooking without this simple, but versatile fruit, which acts as the basis for many sauces, is eaten raw in salads, filled and baked, or made into soup. At the end of summer every year, many families in rural areas preserve their crop: tomatoes are bottled, sun-dried and made into *concentrato*, a thick tomato paste, to be stored away for the year ahead.

4 **sea bream fillets**, about
    200g each
juice of 1 **lemon**
6 tbsp **extra virgin olive oil**, plus
    extra for drizzling
2 **garlic cloves**, finely chopped
1 tbsp **capers**
4 **anchovy fillets**
200ml **white wine**
300g **cherry tomatoes**, deseeded
    and sliced in half
salt and freshly ground **black
    pepper**
150g **black olives**, pitted
a handful of **parsley**, finely
    chopped
a pinch of **oregano**

SERVES 4

CONTALDO

IL DENTICE DI GENNARO
Gennaro's Sea Bream

The reason that this recipe has been named after me is that, while testing recipes for this book, my sister, Adriana, remarked how it included all of my favourite ingredients! I love to cook with garlic, lemon, anchovy, capers, olives, oregano and tomatoes which, I suppose, are the ingredients of my childhood and of the region in which I grew up. I urge you to try it so that you too can see how well these wonderful Mediterranean flavours sing out.

Place the fish fillets in a bowl, squeeze over the lemon juice and leave to marinate for 30 minutes.

Preheat the oven to 200°C/Gas 6.

Heat the olive oil in a large frying pan, add the garlic, capers and anchovy fillets and cook over a medium heat for 5 minutes, until the anchovies have dissolved. Add half of the wine and simmer until it has evaporated, then add the tomatoes, squashing them slightly. Season with salt and pepper and cook for 5 minutes, then add the olives and continue to cook for a further 10 minutes.

Place the fish in an ovenproof dish and season with salt and pepper. Add the parsley, the remaining white wine, the sauce, a drizzle of olive oil and the oregano and cover with foil. Bake in the oven for 20 minutes, removing the foil halfway through cooking.

Remove from the oven, leave to rest for 1 minute then serve with some good country bread.

Carluccio

TONNO ALLA BRACE CON MOLLICA
Grilled Fresh Tuna with Savoury Breadcrumbs

4 **tuna steaks**, about 200g each
salt and freshly ground **black pepper**
juice of 1 **lemon**
1 **lemon**, cut into wedges

SAVOURY BREADCRUMBS
100g fresh **breadcrumbs**
2 **garlic cloves**, crushed
2 tbsp very finely chopped **flat-leaf parsley**
3 tbsp **olive oil**

SERVES 4

This is a very typical recipe from Sicily, where swordfish is sometimes used instead of tuna. The breadcrumb mixture (called muddica _locally) is very common in Sicilian cooking and can be rubbed between the hands to make little pellets like couscous. These breadcrumb pellets can then be used as a replacement for Parmesan on certain types of pasta (thus explaining why it is often referred to as 'poor man's Parmesan'!)._

Preheat a grill – a char-grill would be perfect – or a cast-iron stove-top grill pan.

Mix the breadcrumbs, garlic, parsley and olive oil together in a bowl, using your hands to obtain a dry, mixture. If the mix is too wet, add some more breadcrumbs.

Season the tuna steaks with salt and pepper. Dip each side into the breadcrumb mixture, pressing down lightly, to coat. Squeeze over the lemon juice and cook on the hot grill for 3–4 minutes on each side, until the breadcrumb coating is brown and crispy.

Serve with the lemon wedges and a simple green salad.

4 **trout fillets** (or eel or mackerel)
  about 200g each
plain flour
80ml **olive oil**
1 large **onion**, very finely sliced
50ml **white wine vinegar**

SERVES 4

Carluccio

TROTA IN CARPIONE
Sweet and Sour Marinated Trout

This method of 'curing' fish is northern Italian, and you can find versions from Turin to Venice, all along the Po Valley. The recipe can be made with freshwater fish – abundant in the many rivers and lakes of the north – with eel, or with sea fish. It is commonly eaten as an antipasto or primo, especially on meat-free Fridays, but can be happily served as a main course if accompanied by boiled potatoes and a vegetable or green salad. The dish won't keep for long so eat after marinating or, at the latest, the next day.

FRESHWATER FOOD
Carluccio

Along with miles of coastline, Italy possesses many lakes and rivers, where freshwater fish and shellfish are caught. Trout, eel, pike, perch, carp, catfish, sturgeon and crayfish are all imaginatively cooked. Freshwater fish are also often eaten *in carpione*: fillets of whole fish are dipped in flour, fried and then marinated in a mixture of olive oil and vinegar. The slight sourness achieved (ideal for antipasto), covers the slightly muddy taste that freshwater fish sometimes have.

Frogs also make for exceptionally good (if unexpected) eating. Historically these delicate morsels were a staple diet of the poor in areas such as Vercelli with the legs being particularly good when coated in breadcrumbs and fried in oil. Another favourite (particularly around the Comacchio Valley, south of Venice) is the eel, which can be fried, grilled, baked and stewed.

Dip the fish fillets in the flour to coat, shaking off any excess.

Heat the oil in a large non-stick frying pan. Shallow-fry the fillets, skin-side down first, over a medium heat for about 3–4 minutes on each side until brown. Drain and set aside on kitchen paper.

Add the onion to the same pan and fry in the oil until soft, about 8 minutes. Add the vinegar and boil so that some of the vinegar fumes escape, about 2 minutes.

Arrange the fish in a large dish in one layer, and pour over the hot sauce. Leave to marinate in a cool place for about 6 hours before serving.

CONTALDO

BACCALA E PATATE
Salt Cod and Potatoes

800g *baccalà* (salt cod)
5 tbsp **extra virgin olive oil**
½ **onion**, finely chopped
1 **celery stalk**, finely chopped
½ **red chilli**, finely chopped
400g tinned **plum tomatoes**
a pinch of **oregano**
salt
800g **potatoes**, cut into thick
   chunks

SERVES 4

Baccalà is cod which has been dried and preserved in salt, and it has to be washed and rinsed for two days prior to cooking. Years ago baccalà *used to be part of the poor man's staple diet, especially in the hilly regions where fresh fish was not easily obtainable. Over the years, cod supplies have dwindled and prices have rocketed, making it no longer a poor man's dish but quite the opposite! It is traditional to have* baccalà, *along with other types of fish, on Christmas Eve, enjoyed as fritters or salad (see pages 27 and 108), or baked with potatoes and tomatoes as in this recipe.*

To prepare the *baccalà*, cut into roughly 6cm chunks and place in a large bowl with plenty of cold water. Leave in the fridge to soak for 3 days, changing the water occasionally.

After soaking the fish, bring a saucepan of water to the boil, add the salt cod and cook for about 4 minutes. Remove the fish, drain and place on kitchen paper to dry.

Heat the olive oil in a large pan, add the onion, celery and chilli and sweat until softened. Add the tomatoes, oregano and a little salt to taste (being careful as the cod will be salty) and cook over a medium heat for 10 minutes, until the sauce is silky and smooth.

Add the potatoes, cover the pan and cook over a medium heat for 5 minutes. Add the fish and continue to cook, covered, for a further 10 minutes, until both the fish and potatoes are cooked through and tender. Serve immediately with good country bread.

750g *baccalà* (salt cod)
2 **garlic cloves**, crushed
100g **black olives**, pitted
2 tbsp coarsely chopped
    flat-leaf parsley
6 tbsp **olive oil**
juice of 1½ **lemons**
freshly ground **black pepper**

SERVES 4–6

Carluccio

INSALATA DI BACCALA
Salt Cod Salad

Salt cod is enjoyed all over Italy and is a staple of Catholic Italy, often being eaten during Lent. It was historically very useful for travellers as it could be carried without refrigeration, but nowadays it is mostly eaten because people like its salty taste and flavour – a flavour which this salad embraces.

Cut the fish into chunks, then soak in cold water for 48 hours, changing the water occasionally. (This soaking is best done skin-side up, as it enables the salt to fall to the bottom of the container.)

After soaking the fish, drain it and put it in a pan. Cover with fresh cold water, bring to the boil and cook until soft and flaky, about 20 minutes. Drain, and leave to cool.

Using your fingers, remove all the skin and bones from the salt cod pieces, and reduce the flesh to flakes. Put the fish flakes in a bowl together with the garlic, olives, parsley, olive oil and lemon juice and season with plenty of black pepper. Mix well and serve either on its own or with some good bread.

FAMILY

IN ITALY, FOOD AND FAMILY GO TOGETHER. THE KITCHEN IS THE HEART OF THE HOME WHERE MAMMA ROLLS OUT FRESH PASTA DOUGH, AND NONNA STIRS THE BUBBLING SAUCE ON THE STOVE.
Nonno snoozes in his favourite armchair and a brigade of happy children plays in the courtyard. The traditional Italian family had many children and everyone, even elderly parents, lived together under the same roof. The husband, very much head of the household, went out to work, and his wife stayed at home, in charge of everything else. Over the last 30 years, however, much has changed. Today's modern family consists of parents and perhaps only one or two children. This can be put down to many factors: women are marrying later, preferring to study or further their career before starting a family; the cost of living is so much higher that couples opt for a smaller family, or none at all (with liberalised birth control making such a decision easier); gay men and women are more inclined to 'come out' and are therefore not expected to have children, and divorce is on the increase.

As the demographic of the Italian family has changed, so too have the most basic attitudes to food. Once, girls would have learnt the basics from their mother. Now, with mamma probably out earning a living, many young women have no idea how to cook; they have missed out on what many see as the ultimate intimacy of Italian family, learning to make, say, *tortellini* together. Also, many young career women often do not have the time, or even the desire, to learn how to cook. As a result, pasta is now mass-produced (a boon to the busy), and can be shop-bought. However, all is not lost; it seems that men are now interested in learning how to cook – house-husbands, perhaps, taking over the role of mamma – and there is a growing proliferation of cookery books, television cookery programmes and cookery schools,

all intent on replacing the oral traditions, and keeping the basics of Italian cooking alive.

Due to the speed of modern business life, the style of eating has changed as well. Lunch, once the main meal of the day, is no longer a three-course affair; with working couples, especially in large towns and cities, unable to return home at midday, the main meal is now in the evening, and after a long day at work, no-one wants to cook elaborate dishes any longer. The meal may be a plate of shop-bought pasta with a quick sauce and a salad or some vegetables, or it could be a frittata or steak, which takes little time to prepare. They will rarely serve the full *antipasti*, *primo*, *secondo* and *dolci*.

Older generations, even in the cities, frown upon the new way of eating, and it is not unusual for grandparents to invite their children and grandchildren for lunch on Sunday and special feasts like Christmas, and to cook the traditional three- or four-course meal. I see this with my own family in Italy when my sister cooks for everyone on Sunday. This is the time when families sit together to eat, an unshakeable Italian tradition. It is still unheard of that children eat earlier; even babies are encouraged to join in and taste. And as far as ingredients are concerned, they will be of good quality, and will taste good! Even if some are bought-in rather than home-made, they will be of a quality Italians have been brought up to expect. I firmly believe that, however radically things might change in Italy, the fast-food culture of other countries will never be adopted or accepted.

For Italians still enjoy good, home-cooked food and the favourite topic of conversation is food: when friends meet after being on holiday, the question most often asked is, '*Come avete mangiato*?' (How was the food?), even before asking what the weather was like! A love of food may be inbred in Italians, but one wonders if, with all these changes in family life, it will manage to survive into the next generations. Will they still be making fresh pasta or gnocchi at home in twenty years' time? Will family recipes continue to be passed down from mother to daughter? And what about that special celebration cake nonna made each year for the grandchildren's birthdays? Might it just be easier to go to the *pasticceria* (pastry shop) and buy one?

As in most western countries, life moves on at incredible speed, and families have to adapt. It is no different in Italy, but it would be extremely hard to imagine an Italy without the strong presence of family ties allied with a passion for food.

CONTALDO

4 large **squid**, about 800g
  (cleaned weight)
7 tbsp **olive oil**
2 **garlic cloves**, finely chopped
6 **anchovy fillets** in oil
750g *polpa di pomodoro*
  or chunky passata
salt and freshly ground **black
  pepper**
2 tbsp fresh **oregano**,
  or 1 tsp dried

STUFFING
1 tbsp **olive oil**
about 60g fresh **breadcrumbs**
2 **garlic cloves**, crushed
2 tbsp **pine kernels**
about 50g **Parmesan**, freshly
  grated
2 **eggs**, beaten
2 tbsp chopped fresh **flat-leaf
  parsley**

SERVES 4

Carluccio

CALAMARI RIPIENI ALLA PIZZAIOLA
Stuffed Squid Pizzaiola Style

A squid tube is a natural vessel for a filling, and recipes for stuffed squid are found all around the coastline of Italy. These vary from region to region, but basically consist of breadcrumbs, egg and flavourings. While this once would have been a cucina povera dish for fishermen – using unsold squid and leftovers from the kitchen in the filling – with squid becoming much rarer in the Mediterranean and Adriatic you are now more likely to see this on a fancy restaurant menu instead. In parts of Italy, a variety of squid called 'totano' might be used; this is a large squid with a very long body tube, which makes it ideal for stuffing.

Unless they are already prepared, clean the squid, cutting off the heads and beak. Leave the tubes whole, and keep the little bunches of tentacles together; discard the heads. Remove the transparent quill from each tube, then rinse.

For the stuffing, chop the tentacles very finely and fry them in the oil for about a minute. Drain and put in a bowl. Mix in all the other stuffing ingredients, and season with salt and pepper. Divide the mixture between the squid tubes, leaving a little room at the top, and secure the opening with a wooden cocktail stick.

Heat the olive oil in a large frying pan, add the squid and cook gently for 10–12 minutes. Add the garlic and anchovies, and continue to cook, stirring until the anchovies have almost dissolved into the oil. Add the tomato pulp, salt, pepper and oregano, and stir to combine. This sauce should cover the squid. Cook gently, uncovered, for about 20 minutes. Serve with boiled rice.

CONTALDO

POLLO CASALINGO AL VINO BIANCO
Housewives' Chicken in White Wine and Vinegar

1.2kg **chicken pieces**
  (legs, breasts or thighs,
  whatever you prefer)
600ml **white wine**
3 tbsp **white wine vinegar**
2 **shallots**, finely sliced
2 **carrots,** roughly chopped
1 **celery stalk**, roughly chopped
4 **bay leaves**
2 **cloves**
salt
10 **black peppercorns**
40g **butter**
4 **lemon slices**

SERVES 4

This is an incredibly easy dish to prepare. It comes from Piedmont, and it is said that farmers' wives would prepare all the ingredients in the morning then head off to work in the fields – leaving the chicken to marinate – before coming home and cooking it at night. The combination of vinegar, lemon and cloves gives the chicken a particularly tangy taste.

Place all the ingredients into a large saucepan or casserole. Bring to the boil, lower the heat and cover with a lid, but not completely, so some of the steam can escape. Cook gently for about 50 minutes, turning halfway through, until the chicken pieces have cooked through and are golden-brown on all sides and the liquid has been absorbed. Remove from the heat and serve with rice.

POLLO CON CARCIOFINI, CIPOLLE, PATATE E ROSMARINO
Chicken with Artichokes, Onions, Potatoes and Rosemary

This simple recipe is perfect for a Sunday family lunch. Once prepared and put together, it can be left to the perfect cook, which is the oven! The dish is very versatile – the chicken can be substituted by rabbit (very good indeed), or by any other light meat (slivers of veal, for instance, or even lamb cutlets). Do ensure, however, that you use the tender hearts of baby artichokes – which are available in spring and early summer – as the larger ones will be too tough.

Preheat the oven to 200°C/Gas 6.

Put the chicken pieces, artichokes, onion and potatoes into a large roasting dish. Sprinkle with the rosemary needles, drizzle with olive oil and season with salt and pepper. Mix well with your hands so that every piece of meat is coated well.

Put into the preheated oven for 30 minutes. Take out, mix all the ingredients together well (using a spoon this time!) and return to the oven for another 30 minutes, after which the chicken should be cooked through and the potatoes should be tender.

Serve immediately, finished with a few sprigs of rosemary and accompanied with a simple green salad.

about 8 small **artichokes** (you could use those preserved in water, not brine, which you find in jars), prepared and quartered

1.8kg good-quality **chicken**, cut into chunks

1 large white **onion**, chopped

1kg **new potatoes**, scrubbed and halved or cut into chunks (depending on size)

2 tsp **rosemary needles**, plus a few sprigs for garnish

6 tbsp **olive oil**

salt and freshly ground **black pepper**

SERVES 6

1kg boned **lamb shoulder**, cut into large chunks
salt and freshly ground **black pepper**
10 tbsp **extra virgin olive oil**
2 **onions**, sliced
1 large **carrot**, sliced
1 **celery stalk**, sliced
5 **garlic cloves**, whole and crushed
20g **anchovy fillets**
a handful of **thyme sprigs**
1 **red chilli**, sliced
250ml **white wine**
25ml **white wine vinegar**
250g **fresh or frozen peas**
400g **potatoes**, skins left on and cut into quarters
200g **cherry tomatoes**, halved

SERVES 6

CONTALDO

AGNELLO CON PISELLI FRESCHI
Lamb with Fresh Peas

It is very traditional to eat the new season's lamb with fresh peas at Easter in Italy, and a dish such as this is not uncommon for lunch on Easter Sunday when the whole family will gather together to celebrate one of the most important religious feasts of the year. The secret of success is in leaving the lamb to cook on a very low heat; in this way the lamb and the rest of the ingredients will cook through well, and all the juices will ooze out to create a lovely sauce.

Season the lamb chunks with salt and pepper and set aside.

Heat the olive oil in a large pan and sweat the onions, carrot and celery until soft. Add the garlic, anchovies, thyme and chilli and continue to cook, stirring, until the anchovies have almost dissolved into the oil.

Add the lamb chunks and seal well all over. Stir in the wine and allow to reduce down by about half, then add the vinegar. Reduce the heat to low, cover and simmer gently for 20 minutes. Add the peas, potatoes and tomatoes, cover again and continue to cook for about an hour, until the sauce has reduced by half. Remove from the heat and serve with lots of good toasted bread.

1kg **minced pork**
1 tsp chopped **red chilli**
1 **garlic clove**, finely crushed
1 tsp **fennel seeds**
100ml **red wine**
4 tbsp **olive oil**
salt and freshly ground **black pepper**

SAUCE
2 large **red peppers**
2 large **yellow peppers**
1 tbsp **salted capers**, soaked for 30 minutes, then drained
1 **garlic clove**, sliced
½ **red chilli**, finely chopped
5 **anchovy fillets**
olive oil

SERVES 6

SALSICCE FATTE A MANO CON SALSA PEPOLATA
Hand-made Skinless Sausages with Pepper Sauce

Made from a mixture of minced meat flavoured with a variety of herbs and spices, sausages are very popular in Italy and are often served with polenta. Here I have accompanied them with a 'pepolata' sauce. The name is a combination of peperonata *and* gremolata *and the predominant taste is of roasted peppers – it is also good with grilled meats and fish, or spread on crostini.*

Nothing is easier than producing your own home-made sausages like this, and they can be made with many different meats and spices. My favourite flavourings are fennel seeds, chilli, garlic, red wine, salt and pepper, but you could also use herbs, such as sage, rosemary, oregano, or even basil...

Mix the pork, chilli, garlic, fennel seeds and red wine together in a medium-sized bowl and season with salt and pepper to taste. Using your hands, divide the mixture into twelve and roll each piece into a sausage shape roughly 8cm long and 3cm in diameter.

To prepare the sauce, heat a cast-iron griddle on the hob. Grill the peppers on all sides until the skins are black. Leave to cool a little, then peel off the skin. Cut open and remove the seeds. Put the flesh in a blender with all the other ingredients except the oil, and blend to a purée. Pour in enough oil, stirring all the while, until you have a sauce-like consistency.

Heat the olive oil in a large non-stick pan. Gently place the sausages into the pan and fry over a medium heat until golden on all sides, about 10 minutes. Serve with the sauce.

COSTINE IN UMIDO CON CECI
Slow-cooked Pork Ribs with Chickpeas

This is a robust and rustic dish, typical of cucina povera, *using a cheap cut of meat with a pulse, some herbs from the garden and a home-made tomato sauce. It is simple to prepare and very nutritious. I have used tinned chickpeas here, but if you are using the dried variety, remember to soak them overnight and check the packet for cooking instructions as they can take a long time to cook!*

Heat the olive oil in a large pan, add the onion and sweat until softened. Remove the onion and set aside. Add the ribs to the same pan and seal well on all sides. Return the onion to the pan, add the passata, stock, black pepper and herbs, cover with a lid and simmer gently for 40 minutes. Add the chickpeas and continue to cook, covered, for a further 30 minutes. Taste and adjust for seasoning, if necessary. Remove from the heat and serve with some good country bread.

3 tbsp **olive oil**
1 **onion**, finely chopped
1kg **pork ribs**
400g **passata**
400ml **vegetable stock**
salt and freshly ground **black pepper**
2 sprigs of **thyme**, or a few sage leaves
2 **bay leaves**
400g cooked **chickpeas**

SERVES 6

Carluccio

SCOTTIGLIA CON POLENTA ALLA SPIANATORA
Mixed Meat Stew with Polenta

This dish combines various ingredients and ideas typical of three regions, while still maintaining the essential Italian style. Polenta is from the north, the scottiglia *is a stew of various meats typical of Tuscany, and the way of eating the dish comes from the Abruzzi. 'Alla spianatora' refers to the special round table or board of the Abruzzi on which cooked wet polenta is spread, with a mound of stew in the middle. People sit around the table, armed with forks, and tuck in – it's a really sociable meal.*

First, prepare the stew. Cut the meats into walnut-sized pieces. Heat the oil in a large pan and add the vegetables and garlic. Sauté until soft, about 7 minutes, then add the meat. Let it brown slightly on all sides, about 8–10 minutes, then add the wine and lower the heat to a simmer. Add the juniper berries, peppercorns, sage, rosemary and tomato pulp and cook for 5 minutes or so, then add the nutmeg and the tomato purée. Cook, uncovered, for a further hour, until the meat is tender. Season with salt and pepper to taste.

When the meat is nearly ready, start to prepare the polenta. Bring the water to the boil in a large pan, with the salt added. Pour in the polenta and cook, stirring, for a few minutes, until thickened and smooth, about 5 minutes. (Be careful not to burn yourself when the mixture bubbles volcanically.) Add the cheeses and the butter, and stir vigorously, off the heat. Keep warm over a very low heat.

Get everyone to the table. Spread the polenta on to your chosen board or table, making a well in the middle. Taste the stew for seasoning again, then pour into the middle of the polenta. *Buon appetito!*

2.2kg **mixed meats** like pork, lamb or wild boar, if available
100ml **olive oil**
4 **celery stalks**, very finely diced
1 large **onion**, finely chopped
2 large **carrots**, very finely diced
3 **garlic cloves**, finely chopped
200ml **red wine**
1 tbsp **juniper berries**
1 tsp whole **black peppercorns**
4 **sage leaves**
1 tbsp **rosemary needles**
1.5kg *polpa di pomodoro* or chunky passata
1 tsp freshly grated **nutmeg**
2 tbsp **tomato purée**
salt and freshly ground **black pepper**

POLENTA CONCIA
3 litres **water**
20g **salt**
600g **quick-cook polenta**
120g **Fontina cheese** (or Taleggio), freshly grated
80g **Parmesan**, freshly grated
100g **unsalted butter**

SERVES 10

5 tbsp **extra virgin olive oil**
1 small **onion**, finely chopped
500g **topside of beef**, chopped
   into medium-sized chunks
500g **pork ribs**
200g **Italian pork sausages**
2 tbsp **tomato concentrate**,
   diluted in 100ml red wine
3 x 400g tins **chopped tomatoes**
a handful of **basil leaves**
salt and freshly ground **black**
   pepper

SERVES 4–6

PORK *Carluccio*

The most important friend of the Italians
in a culinary sense is the pig. After killing
one (usually between November and
January) the family will have sustenance
for the entire year. The animal is divided
into various parts, with nothing thrown
away. The offal is eaten fresh, as is a
proportion of the flesh (loin, chops, leg,
ribs and sausages such as *luganiga*). The
blood is used in black puddings, and
even in a sweet tart in the south. The legs
become cured hams, while part of the
head, ears and tail are used in *cotechino*,
a gelatinous sausage, and the trotters in a
dish called *zampone*. The fat is rendered,
to be used as lard, with the resulting
ciccioli (pork scratchings) eaten as bread.
   The fresh meat is also preserved, salted
and dried, to make salami and other
cured items, such as pancetta (belly pork
bacon), *coppa* (neck), *guanciale* (cheeks)
and *mortadella*.

CONTALDO

IL RAGU DI GENNARO
Gennaro's Mixed Meat Ragù

*This has to be my favourite dish, as it's so reminiscent of my
childhood. Historically meat* ragù *was slow-cooked in terracotta
pots for up to 12 hours, which may seem absurd, but believe me the
taste was amazing.* Ragù *is the traditional Sunday lunch for most
southern Italian families: the tomato sauce dresses the pasta and the
meat is served as a main course.* Ragù *is so popular that it is even
featured in a 1990 Sophia Loren film,* Saturday, Sunday, Monday.
*In one scene Sophia goes to the butcher and ends up in quite a fiery
discussion with other housewives as to what makes the perfect* ragù!
*I dedicate this recipe to my mother, Zia Maria, and my sisters who
themselves have never stopped arguing about this incredible dish…*

Heat the olive oil in a large saucepan, add the onion and cook until
softened. Add the beef, ribs and sausages and seal well all over (you
may need to do this in batches). Raise the heat, stir in the diluted
tomato concentrate and reduce by a third. Add the tomatoes and basil,
season with salt and pepper and stir well. Bring to the boil, then lower
the heat to a simmer, cover and cook very gently for about 2 hours,
until the sauce is thick and silky. Stir from time to time, checking that
there is enough moisture; if necessary add a little more wine or water.

Remove from the heat and serve with pasta as suggested above, or on
its own with lots of good bread to mop up the rich tomato sauce.

6 tbsp **extra virgin olive oil**
100g **pancetta** or bacon, roughly
  chopped
800g **pork fillet**
2 **garlic cloves**, left whole
4 tbsp **honey**
12g **ginger**, peeled and
  finely sliced
2 **carrots**, roughly chopped
4 baby **parsnips**, peeled and
  cut in half, or 500g pumpkin,
  peeled and sliced
4 **shallots**, halved or quartered,
  depending on size
2 sprigs of **rosemary**
300ml **vegetable stock**
freshly ground **black pepper**

SERVES 4–6

CONTALDO

LONZA AL MIELE E ZENZERO
Pork Fillet with Honey and Ginger

Dishes using slightly more exotic ingredients are becoming popular in Italy now. People are experimenting with more unusual spices as they become more readily available, especially in cities, probably because this is where immigrants have settled. This is a really simple way of cooking pork and the addition of honey and ginger (the unusual ingredient here) gives the meat a flavoursome kick!

Heat the olive oil in a large saucepan and fry the pancetta until golden. Remove from the pan and set aside.

In the same pan, add the pork and seal on all sides. Now add the garlic, honey and ginger and continue to cook over a medium heat until caramelised. Add the carrots, parsnips or pumpkin, shallots, rosemary, pancetta, stock and black pepper, cover with a lid and cook on a medium to low heat for 30 minutes. Check the vegetables are tender, remove and set aside. Continue to cook the meat until tender and cooked through, about another hour, before removing from the pan and setting aside. Leave the pork fillet to cool slightly, before cutting into thick slices.

Return both the vegetables and the pork slices to the pan to heat through before serving.

Carluccio

POLPETTONE
Meatloaf with Tomatoes

Probably the cheapest of all the meat dishes in this chapter, this is very much a family dish, typically cooked when there is not very much money and there are many hungry mouths to feed. It is served in much the same way as Gennaro's Mixed Meat Ragù *(see page 124) – the juices with pasta first, then the meat, in slices, as a main course. Two dishes for the price of one, then.*

Mix the meats, eggs, nutmeg, breadcrumbs and the Parmesan together in a large bowl and season with salt and pepper. Mix well together, then shape into a nice oval shape with your hands and place on a piece of foil.

In a very large pan or casserole dish, heat the olive oil. Gently lift the meatloaf into the pan and brown all over. Turn it gently so as not to break it. Add the chopped onions and fry until soft, about 10 minutes. Pour in the white wine, and cook to let the alcohol evaporate, then add the tomato pulp until the loaf is covered (adding a little extra water if necessary). Cover with a lid and simmer on a very low heat, for about 1½ hours. Check from time to time: if it looks as if it needs additional moisture, add a little water. Season with salt and pepper to taste.

Lift the meatloaf carefully from the pan, and cut into thick slices. Serve with pasta in the same way as *Gennaro's Mixed Meat Ragù* (see page 124).

500g **minced beef**
250g **minced pork**
250g **minced veal**
4 **eggs**, beaten
½ tsp freshly grated **nutmeg**
75g fresh **breadcrumbs**
75g **Parmesan**, freshly grated, plus extra for sprinkling
salt and freshly ground **black pepper**
8 tbsp **olive oil**
2 large **onions**, finely chopped
75ml dry **white wine**
4 x 400g tins *polpa di pomodoro* or chunky passata

SERVES 4

Carluccio

OSSO BUCO IN BIANCO
Braised Veal Shanks

Osso buco *literally means 'bone with hole'. The name refers to the cut, from veal shanks or shin, which always include the bone; this contains marrow, and is an important part of the dish. Osso buco is a speciality of Milan, where its traditional accompaniment is risotto milanese (see page 85). This is the original version, made without tomatoes, and now known as* osso buco in bianco. *There has been a trend lately to include tomatoes in the stew, which makes for a dish that is better accompanied by potatoes or polenta.*

Coat the meat in flour and season with salt and pepper. Heat the oil in a large pan, add the veal and fry until browned on both sides, about 5–6 minutes on each side. Set aside.

Add the onion, carrots, celery and bay leaves to the same pan and fry until the onion is softened, about 8 minutes. Pour in the wine and allow to evaporate slightly, then add the meat, stock, sage, rosemary and orange zest. Bring to the simmer, then cover and cook gently for about 1½ hours, until the meat is tender. Check from time to time and add a little more stock if the mixture is getting too dry.

Season to taste and serve with *Risotto Milanese* (see page 85). Enjoy!

4 x 5cm thick slices **veal shin**, about 1kg
plain flour, for coating
salt and freshly ground **black pepper**
6 tbsp **olive oil**
1 large **onion**, finely chopped
2 **carrots**, very finely diced
3 **celery stalks**, very finely diced
4 **bay leaves**
100ml dry **white wine**
1 litre **beef or chicken stock** (see page 38)
4 **sage leaves**
1 sprig of **rosemary**
grated zest of 1 small **orange**

SERVES 4

SECONDI **129**

1kg **pork belly**, not too fatty,
  cut into 4 slices
salt and freshly ground **black
  pepper**
1 **celery stalk**
1 **carrot**
80ml **crème fraîche**, to serve

SAUERKRAUT
2 tbsp **olive oil**
1 **onion**, chopped
800g **sauerkraut** (available in jars
  from good delicatessens)
80ml **apple juice**
2 tsp **caster sugar**
1 tsp **juniper berries**
1 tsp **black peppercorns**
2–3 **bay leaves**

SERVES 4

Carluccio

PANCETTA CON CRAUTI
Pork Belly with Sauerkraut

*This recipe hails from Croatia originally, but is also eaten in
Germany and Austria (where it is known as Szegediner gulasch)
as well as in the Italian Südtirol, in Friuli and Trieste. Undoubtedly
a cucina povera dish, it is very hearty, making delicious use of the
cheap cut of pork and the preserved cabbage, which is the defining
vegetable taste of this whole geographic area.*

Put the pork belly slices in a suitable pan, cover with lightly salted
water and add the celery and carrot. Bring to the boil, then reduce the
heat to a simmer and cook for 2 hours, until the meat is tender.

After an hour, start preparing the sauerkraut. Heat the olive oil in
another pan, add the onion and fry until soft, about 7 minutes. Add
the sauerkraut, apple juice, sugar, juniper berries, peppercorns and bay
leaves and season with salt and pepper. Bring to the boil, then reduce
the heat to a simmer and cook for an hour until the cabbage is tender.
If it looks like it needs more liquid, add a little more water (though it
should be fairly dryish at the end).

Take the belly pork out of the hot water and drain, discarding the
vegetables. Cut the pork slices into chunks and cubes, and mix with
the sauerkraut. Serve topped with crème fraîche.

Carluccio

CAPRETTO CON UOVA E LIMONE
Kid with Egg and Lemon Sauce

Usually cooked at Easter, this dish shows a Greek influence in the use of the egg and lemon sauce – avgolemono in Greek – which has been happily adopted in the south of Italy. Lamb can, of course, be substituted for the kid, should you wish.

Coat the meat in flour on all sides, shaking off any excess, and season with salt and pepper. Heat the oil in a large pan, add the kid and fry until browned on both sides, about 15 minutes. Add the wine and cook gently for 10–15 minutes, stirring from time to time, until the meat is tender. If it looks as if it needs additional moisture, add a little extra water or stock.

Meanwhile, beat the egg yolks and eggs together in a bowl. Add the lemon juice, garlic and parsley, and season with salt and pepper.

Take the meat pan off the heat and, while still warm, but not too hot, add the egg mixture. Stir to coat all the pieces of meat with sauce: the sauce should just thicken without becoming scrambled egg (it's a similar process to *spaghetti carbonara*). Serve with buttered spinach, boiled potatoes or some good bread.

about 1kg **kid**, cut into 5cm
   pieces
plain flour, for coating
salt and freshly ground **black
   pepper**
6 tbsp **olive oil**
50ml dry **white wine**

SAUCE
3 **egg yolks**
3 whole **eggs**
juice of 1½ **lemons**
2 **garlic cloves**, finely crushed
1 tbsp chopped **flat-leaf parsley**

SERVES 4

juice and grated zest of ½ **orange**

juice and grated zest of ½ **lemon**

7 tbsp **extra virgin olive oil**

½ **garlic clove**, finely chopped

4 sprigs of **thyme**

1 **rabbit**, about 1kg, cut into pieces

2 **shallots**, finely chopped

50ml **white wine**

salt and freshly ground **black pepper**

80g pitted **black olives**

a little **vegetable stock**, if necessary

SERVES 4

CONTALDO

CONIGLIO CON OLIVE, TIMO E MARINATA DI AGRUMI
Citrus-marinated Rabbit with Black Olives and Thyme

This is a simple-to-prepare country dish, with wonderful fresh ingredients. The infusion of citrus fruits and fresh thyme and the saltiness of the olives marry very well with the rabbit's delicate flesh. Serve with some good country bread and a crunchy salad of fennel, or with polenta concia *(see page 121), as pictured here. If you prefer, you can replace the rabbit with good-quality organic chicken.*

In a bowl, combine the orange juice and zest, lemon juice and zest, 4 tablespoons of the olive oil, garlic and thyme in a bowl. Pour this over the rabbit pieces and leave to marinate for 45 minutes.

Heat the remaining olive oil in a large frying pan, add the shallots and sweat until softened. Remove the rabbit pieces from the marinade (ensuring you reserve it) add to the pan and seal well on all sides. Pour in the wine and cook, stirring, until it evaporates. Lower the heat, pour in the marinade and season with salt and pepper. Cover with a lid and cook gently for 15 minutes. Add the olives and cook for a further 15 minutes, until the rabbit is tender. Stir from time to time, checking that there is enough moisture; if necessary add a little vegetable stock.

Remove from the heat, check for seasoning and serve immediately.

CONTORNI
VEGETABLES

THE TYPICAL MEAT AND TWO VEG MENTALITY DOESN'T APPLY TO ITALIAN MAIN COURSES. Often only one vegetable will accompany a main course meat or fish, perhaps with or instead of a salad. But these too, like in all the other courses, have to be of the best quality and very carefully cooked, in an imaginative way, to maximise tastiness.

As well as being seasonal, the vegetables will be extremely local, and at one time, home-grown produce would have formed the major part of what the locals ate. Even the humblest of vegetables – potatoes, beans, cabbage, carrots – when accompanied by olive oil, garlic and perhaps some ricotta cheese, eaten with bread or polenta, would give enough sustenance to keep people going. However, in the last 30 to 40 years, vegetables (and fruit) from the south have started being delivered to the north overnight via lorry from regions such as Puglia, Calabria and Sicily, where the warm season starts earlier. This not only satisfies the tastes of southerners now living in the north, but has resulted in many of the vegetables being adopted into the local northern cuisines.

CONTALDO
Italians tend to eat vegetables in season, and in most smaller towns and villages this is exactly what happens. It would be unheard of to eat asparagus in winter or pumpkin in spring! It is also good to anticipate the arrival of the first peas or broad beans in spring, fresh from their pods, or the beloved San Marzano tomatoes at the end of summer.

Italian vegetables are never plainly boiled and served: we like to add flavour, even if only with extra virgin olive oil, and perhaps lemon juice or wine or balsamic vinegar, depending on taste and the type of vegetable. Herbs add a great deal of flavour to the simplest dishes as well: think of steamed courgettes or green beans, with olive oil, lemon, mint and garlic. Vegetables can be sautéed in oil, garlic and chilli, baked in the oven with a cheese or breadcrumb topping, roasted with herbs or dipped in batter and deep-fried. The options are endless and always delicious.

Salads too are popular. Escarole, endive, watercress, rocket, dandelion and radicchio are just a few of the leaves that might go into a classic salad, simply dressed with the best olive oil and lemon juice. In season, young raw broad beans are eaten with shavings of pecorino cheese, while baby courgettes are thinly sliced and dressed with oil, lemon juice and fresh mint, and tomatoes and basil make for an unforgettable – and uniquely Italian – combination.

400g **green beans**, trimmed
salt and freshly ground **black pepper**
100g **unsalted butter**
6 tbsp **dried breadcrumbs** (see page 154)
1 tbsp **pine nuts**

SERVES 4

FAGIOLINI E COMPAGNI
Green Beans, Buttered Breadcrumbs and Pine Nuts

This recipe translates as 'green beans and co.' and is a very refreshing accompaniment to any meats or fish, or by itself. It's not a classic, but a modern invention of mine, using basically just three ingredients. It is however very Italian in essence, and who knows, perhaps it might even become a classic…

Put the beans in a saucepan of lightly salted boiling water and cook until tender, at least 10 minutes.

In another suitable pan, melt the butter over a high heat, add the breadcrumbs and pine nuts and fry until the crumbs are brown, a few minutes only. Stir all the time with a wooden spoon.

Drain the beans, place in a flat serving dish, and sprinkle the breadcrumb mixture over the top. Season to taste and serve.

8 small **Romanesco artichokes**
juice of 1 small **lemon**
300ml **olive oil**
salt and freshly ground **black
  pepper**

SERVES 4

CARCIOFI ALLA GIUDEA
Jewish Fried Artichokes

This recipe originated from the Jewish ghetto in Rome and is traditionally eaten during Pesach, *the Jewish equivalent of Easter, when artichokes are in season. If you find yourself in Rome in the Jewish quarter then I strongly recommend you visit the restaurants and sample this simple but delicious dish. For this recipe you should use the small, violet Romanesco artichokes.*

With a small, sharp knife, remove the bottom outer leaves of each artichoke and scrape the stems from top to bottom. Trim the stem slightly and cut the tips off the leaves with a small sharp knife.

Place the prepared artichokes in a bowl of water mixed with lemon juice until ready to use.

Heat the oil in a large, deep pan. Remove the artichokes from the water and drain well. Season the artichokes, then add them to the pan side-by-side and stalk-side up. Pack them in tightly so they don't wobble during cooking. The oil should come three-quarters of the way up the artichokes, so if necessary add some more. Reduce the heat to medium and cook the artichokes for about 15 minutes until tender, turning them from time to time so they cook evenly. Increase the heat, turn the artichokes the original way (stalk-side up) and press firmly with a wooden spoon so the leaves spread out and the artichokes resemble flattened flowers. Cook for a further 5 minutes, until golden.

Remove from the heat, drain well on kitchen paper and serve immediately with a sprinkling of salt if desired.

3 large **red peppers**, seeded and
  cut into strips
3 large **yellow peppers**, seeded
  and cut into strips
2 **white onions**, sliced
2 **garlic cloves**, finely chopped
500g **plum tomatoes**, cut into
  chunks
6 tbsp **olive oil**
4 tbsp *polpa di pomodoro*
  or chunky passata (optional)
salt and freshly ground **black
  pepper**

SERVES 4–6

PEPERONATA
Pepper, Tomato and Onion Stew

This dish – a Piedmontese speciality, locally known as puvruna *– is
a vegetable stew much like the French* ratatouille *and the southern
Italian* caponata. *Here the ingredients are peppers, tomatoes and
onions; often the peppers used are the square, large peppers of
Carmagnola, which come in a multitude of colours (even black),
and are often eaten, cut into strips and dipped into the Piedmontese
anchovy and butter sauce, known as* bagna cauda. *This stew can
be eaten as an accompaniment to any sort of food, meat or fish, but
can also be enjoyed as part of an antipasti platter.*

Put the pepper strips, onion slices, garlic and tomatoes in a pan with
the oil. If the tomatoes are not fully ripe, add the tomato pulp to
loosen the mixture. Put the lid on the pan and bring to the boil, then
reduce the heat and simmer for 10 minutes. Add salt and pepper to
taste, and cook for another 20 minutes. Eat warm or leave to cool
before serving.

about 600g **purple sprouting broccoli**, calabrese or *cime di rapa*
salt and freshly ground **black pepper**
6 tbsp **olive oil**
2 **garlic cloves**, very finely chopped
1 tbsp very finely chopped **red chilli**
juice of ½ **lemon**

SERVES 4

BROCCOLETTI SALTATI
Sautéed Broccoli Spears

This is a very typical southern dish. Traditionally bitter wild greens such as cime di rapa *(a brassica, with flowering tops similar to broccoli) would be used in this recipe – and I have occasionally made it with the young rape tops that I have plucked from a neighbouring farmer's fields before they turn their wonderful golden colour. Should you not find wild greens so easy to come by, you can always substitute purple sprouting broccoli or calabrese broccoli instead.*

Trim the broccoli, cutting off the tougher ends of the stem. If using calabrese, break into florets.

Bring a large pan of lightly salted boiling water to the boil. Add the broccoli and cook for 8–9 minutes, until tender. Drain and set aside.

Heat the oil in a large frying pan and fry the garlic and chilli for about 1 minute. Add the broccoli and cook very briefly, stirring, for about 30 seconds. Squeeze over the lemon juice and season with salt and pepper. Serve immediately.

PURE DI CAROTE E SEDANO RAPA
Carrot and Celeriac Purée

I used to serve this in my restaurant and it is more of an idea really than a proper recipe: a combination of vegetables providing different colours, flavours and textures. It can be used to accompany almost anything, meat or fish and is a perfect winter dish to serve with a family roast on a Sunday.

Put the carrots, celeriac and potatoes in a large saucepan of lightly salted boiling water and cook together until soft, about 30–40 minutes. Remove from the heat and drain well.

Mash the vegetables together, using a masher, then blend in a food processor until fine, about 5 minutes. (Because of the quantities involved you may need to do this in batches.) Add the nutmeg and butter and season to taste. Serve hot.

600g **carrots**, diced
600g **celeriac**, diced
200g **potatoes**, diced
salt and freshly ground **black pepper**
a pinch of freshly grated **nutmeg**
60g **unsalted butter**

SERVES 4

7 tbsp **extra virgin olive oil**
500g **potatoes**, thinly sliced
1 tsp dried **oregano**
salt and freshly ground **black pepper**
a large handful of **basil leaves**, roughly torn
300g **red onions**, sliced
400g **cherry tomatoes**, halved and deseeded
1 tbsp **white wine**

SERVES 4

CONTALDO

PATATE ARRAGANATE
Sliced Roasted Potatoes with Tomato, Oregano and Basil

This is a wonderful accompaniment to meat or fish dishes, and, if you increase the quantities, makes a lovely main course in itself when served with a salad. Arraganate means 'with oregano', and this herb infuses wonderfully with the potatoes and tomatoes during roasting. Whenever I make this dish the whole house is filled with a wonderful aroma of oregano and basil, transporting me right back to the Mediterranean.

Preheat the oven to 180°C/Gas 4.

Pour 3 tablespoons of the olive oil into an ovenproof dish or roasting tin. Arrange a layer of the potatoes, sprinkle over a little of the oregano, season with salt and pepper and scatter over some basil leaves. Follow with a layer of onions and tomatoes and a drizzle of the remaining olive oil. Continue with another layer of potatoes and repeat the process until all the vegetables have been added to the dish. Pour over the remaining olive oil and white wine.

Cover with foil and bake in the oven for 45 minutes. Remove the foil and loosen the potatoes from the bottom of the dish with a fork, taking care not to break them. Continue to bake for a further 15–20 minutes, until the potatoes are cooked through. Serve immediately.

600g **baby courgettes**
olive oil, for deep-frying
salt and freshly ground **black
  pepper**

BATTER
2 tbsp **plain flour**
2 **eggs**, beaten

SERVES 4

ZUCCHINI FRITTI
Deep-fried Courgette Matchsticks

Courgettes are probably the most used vegetable in Italy, although they are not given the praise that I think they deserve. The Italians are reputed to have developed this smaller version of the vegetable marrow – or at least encouraged an appreciation of it – at some point in the 19th century. Though the courgette may be humble, it produces wonderful results. It can be eaten raw, fried in slices, baked or grilled whole, stuffed, included in both lasagne and parmigiani or deep-fried, as below.

Top and tail the courgettes and cut them in half lengthways. Cut out the white centre and seeds, if there are any, (this part is too watery for frying), and slice the the remainder into batons. Cut these in half widthways so that you are left with matchsticks about 5cm long.

Heat the oil in a large, deep pan until slightly smoking.

Meanwhile, mix the flour and eggs together to make a light batter. Season with salt and pepper. Dip a handful of the courgette matchsticks into the batter, then plunge them into the hot oil. Deep-fry in batches, separating them with a spoon, until they crisp, about 4–5 minutes. Drain well on kitchen paper.

Sprinkle with salt and pepper and serve immediately.

CUCINA POVERA

IN MOST WESTERN COUNTRIES, THERE WERE AND ARE DIFFERENT STYLES OF COOKING, PRINCIPALLY THOSE EMPLOYED BY THE RICH – IN ITALY THIS IS KNOWN AS *CUCINA RICCA* – AND THOSE OF THE POOR, *CUCINA POVERA*.

Cucina povera is the food the poor of Italy used to cook, dictated by the limited number of ingredients available to them. Grain-based foods such as pasta, bread, polenta and gnocchi were staples of *cucina povera*, as was rice, with beans and pulses instead providing much-needed protein, and vegetables and fruit (probably gathered from the wild) would be basic nutrients. Meat appears only occasionally in *cucina povera* – in the country, animals would be too valuable as milk- or egg-suppliers, and in the cities, meat would have been far too expensive – with most meat dishes originating from the unwanted animal offal rejected by the grand banqueting halls of the rich.

Because poor people had so little to draw on in the way of ingredients, they learnt to value their quality, to cook them lovingly in order to make them taste delicious – and to make them go as far as they could. They also learned to preserve any food they had available, by salting, drying, or a combination, and a major strand of Italian cooking is based on these *cucina povera* principles: think of all the preserved vegetables, the salami, the sausages, the hams. Fish, too, were salted or dried – *baccalà* (salt cod), for instance – so that they could be kept for long periods of time. These types of preserved foods were ideal food for the poor, but frowned upon by the rich. Now most people can only afford to buy *baccalà* at Christmas – how times have changed!

Pulses of all varieties are widely used in the Italian kitchen and this certainly dates back to the times when meat prices were prohibitive: think of the many bean-based soups. They have become even more popular over recent years and some varieties, such as the Castelluccio lentils of Umbria, command huge prices. Grains were vital too, and *primi* dishes such as eggless pasta, polenta and gnocchi were foods of the poor: pasta was eaten mainly in the south, polenta and rice in the north, and gnocchi throughout. Sauces for these foods would be concocted from what was available – a glut of courgettes, say, or a lucky haul of shellfish. One type of pasta stands out to me, the *birboni*, made in Campania. Leftover white and wholemeal flour, which ended up on the floor of the pasta factories, at the end of the working day would be swept up, mixed with water and used to make tagliatelle-like pasta shapes.

Bread was another grain-based food used in many *cucina povera* dishes, and would be baked or bought every day. Even when stale it would not be wasted – day-old bread was used in the famous Tuscan bread salad, *panzanella*, and in the Puglian dish of *pane cotto e patate* (bread and potatoes). Breadcrumbs would coat many foods to be fried, and be made into *polpette* (dumplings). These would be served either in a broth or with tomato sauce. Interesting breads from Puglia and Campania, with added bits and pieces from housewives' leftovers such as salami and cheese rind, were made as a nutritious lunch for their husbands working in the fields.

Cucina povera was a tradition and way of life, and it is still very much alive today. The sheer simplicity and tastiness of many of these dishes never ceases to amaze me, and they give a great insight into the resourcefulness of those for whom it was the only possible way of cooking. Indeed, in recent years, this style of cooking has become very fashionable and can now be seen on the menus of the best restaurants across the globe. From being something that was looked down upon, *cucina povera* has almost become the aspirational food of the rich. And for these recipes to still be enjoyed today at home, and also served in top restaurants worldwide, is a sign that the poor of years ago actually ate very well!

CONTALDO

about 4 large **fennel bulbs**,
   trimmed and halved
salt and freshly ground **black
   pepper**
75g **unsalted butter**
½ tsp freshly grated **nutmeg**
4 tbsp **dried breadcrumbs**
   (see p154)
4 tbsp freshly grated **Parmesan**

SERVES 4

Carluccio

FINOCCHI GRATINATI
Fennel Gratin

*The Italians were responsible for developing fennel from the wild
herbal plant (still valued for its stalks and seeds), in the 17th
century. It is a wonderful vegetable – very good raw in salads, eaten
as a digestif after a meal, or baked to use as an accompaniment or
side dish for fish and lighter meat dishes, as here. An ideal way of
using up stale bread, breadcrumbs are used a lot in Italian cooking,
and the grilled crisp breadcrumb topping here creates a wonderful
contrast of texture with the soft fennel underneath.*

Preheat the oven to 180°C/Gas 4.

Cook the fennel halves in lightly salted water for about 20 minutes,
until soft. Drain and leave to cool slightly before cutting into 1cm
slices lengthways (you should get roughly three slices per half bulb).

Grease a medium baking dish with 15g of the butter and arrange the
fennel slices in it, overlapping each other, like roof tiles. Sprinkle over
the nutmeg, breadcrumbs and Parmesan and season with salt and
pepper. Dot the remaining butter over the top.

Bake in the oven until the breadcrumbs and Parmesan start to brown
and the edges have become crisp, about 15 minutes. Serve hot.

CONTALDO

MELANZANE RIPIENE AL FORNO
Baked Stuffed Aubergines

Aubergines are a typical and extremely versatile Southern Italian vegetable that grow in abundance during the summer and can be enjoyed simply grilled, made into the famous melanzane alla parmigiana, *preserved in oil and served as an antipasto, used in pasta sauces or filled and baked as in this recipe. This dish makes a lovely accompaniment, but is also substantial enough to be served with a salad and enjoyed as a main course.*

Preheat the oven to 220°C/Gas 7.

Cut the aubergines in half lengthways to give 8 halves. Take 6 of the aubergine halves and make an incision with a small sharp knife about ½cm in from the edge, taking care not to tear the skin. Carefully remove the pulp with a spoon. You will be left with empty aubergine shells resembling boats. Finely chop the pulp and set aside. Peel the remaining 2 aubergine halves, discard the skin and finely chop the flesh, then add to the rest of the pulp.

Heat the oil in a large frying pan, add the onion and sweat until softened. Add the pulp and cook over a medium heat for about 4 minutes, stirring all the time. Add the tomatoes, basil, salt and pepper, and cook for a further 2 minutes, stirring, until soft. Remove from the heat and leave to cool, then mix in the bread, provolone and 3 tablespoons of the Parmesan. Fill the aubergine shells with this mixture.

Drizzle a little olive oil in an ovenproof dish and place the filled shells in it, ensuring they are packed together tightly. Top with the cherry tomatoes and drizzle over a little more oil. Mix together the dried breadcrumbs and the remaining Parmesan and sprinkle over each one.

Bake in the oven for 20–25 minutes until golden-brown. Serve hot.

4 large **aubergines**
150ml **extra virgin olive oil**, plus extra for drizzling
1 **onion**, finely chopped
250g **tomatoes**, roughly chopped
handful of **basil leaves**, roughly torn
salt and freshly ground **black pepper**
100g **bread**, roughly cut into cubes and crumbled
120g **provolone cheese**, cut into very small cubes
5 tbsp freshly grated **Parmesan**

TOPPING
12 **cherry tomatoes**, sliced
2 tbsp **dried breadcumbs** (see page 154)

SERVES 4

80g **dried breadcrumbs**
  (see below)
1 **garlic clove**, very finely
  chopped
1 sprig **rosemary needles**, very
  finely chopped
salt and freshly ground **black
  pepper**
600g **pumpkin**
plain flour, for dusting
abundant **sunflower oil**, for
  frying

SERVES 4

ZUCCA CON LE BRICIOLE
Pumpkin Chips with Tangy Breadcrumbs

Pumpkin was traditionally very common among rural communities throughout Italy, where it would be made into pasta dishes, soups, stews, risottos, gnocchi or simply sautéed. Here I have given it a modern twist and transformed it into chips topped with a tangy breadcrumb topping, though you could simply sprinkle it with some salt, black pepper, some chopped rosemary or even chilli powder if you prefer. It is great as a side dish, as a snack for children or even served at parties.

In a small bowl, combine the breadcrumbs, garlic, rosemary and a little salt and pepper. Set aside.

Cut the pumpkin into 2–3mm slices and dust in flour, shaking off any excess. Pour enough sunflower oil into a frying pan to cover the base generously, add the pumpkin slices and fry for a couple of minutes until golden. Remove and drain on kitchen paper. Place on a plate, sprinkle over the breadcrumb topping and serve.

BRICIOLE
Dried Breadcrumbs

To make the breadcrumbs, place some sliced stale bread on a baking tray and bake in the oven at 120°C/Gas ½ for about an hour to dry out completely. Remove from the oven and chop very finely or whiz in a food processor. Store in an airtight container until needed.

1kg small **white onions**, peeled
salt
3 tbsp **olive oil**
2 tbsp **caster sugar**
3 tbsp **balsamic vinegar**

MAKES 1 KG

BALSAMIC VINEGAR
Carluccio

Balsamic vinegar has a unique taste, flavour and texture. Made from the white Trebbiano grape, by law it can be produced only in the province of Modena in Emilia-Romagna. *Balsamico tradizionale* is produced by a handful of Emilian families – aged for up to 50 years, it is very expensive. To produce it, the grape must is matured in a series of barrels of different woods each year which are kept under the roof, where the temperature extremes encourage evaporation, so intensifying flavour.

This very old and expensive *balsamico* is used in drops (lovely on a chunk of Parmesan) to flavour fish, meat and even strawberries, but never on salad (unless you are a millionaire!). Cheaper balsamics are simply ordinary vinegar with the addition of burnt sugar.

CIPOLLINE IN AGRODOLCE BALSAMICO
Sweet and Sour Baby Onions with Balsamic Vinegar

Italians love the tart taste of pickled vegetables – mushrooms, artichokes, olives, gherkins and, of course, little onions – as accompaniments or as antipasti. The onions typically used in this dish are of a variety that is slightly smaller than pickling onions, which are available seasonally and regionally throughout the whole of Italy. This is not a lasting pickle: either serve immediately or keep until the next day, no longer.

Boil the small onions in salted water for about 20 minutes, or until soft. Drain well.

Put the olive oil in a large, deep-sided frying pan, add the onions and fry for about 10 minutes over a medium heat. Add the sugar and vinegar, and fry for another 5 minutes or so, stirring, so that all the onions are evenly coated with the flavouring.

Serve hot or cold as an antipasto or side dish.

CONTALDO

INSALATA DI FINOCCHI E SCAMORZA
Fennel and Scamorza Cheese Salad

4 tbsp **extra virgin olive oil**
juice of **1 lemon**
1 tsp **mustard powder**
1 sprig of **thyme leaves**
salt and freshly ground **black pepper**
2 **fennel bulbs**, trimmed and finely sliced
150g **Scamorza or hard mozzarella**, sliced into thick matchsticks

SERVES 4

A very simple recipe which combines the softness of the cheese and crunchiness of the fennel. Scamorza, a hard, firm cheese similar to mozzarella is very popular in the Campania region, but not easily found elsewhere: try a good Italian delicatessen.

Combine the olive oil, lemon juice, mustard, thyme and a little salt and pepper in a small bowl. Arrange the fennel and cheese slices on a plate, drizzle over the dressing and serve.

250g **fresh or frozen broad beans**
50g **walnuts**
½ **garlic clove**
¼ **red chilli**
4 tbsp **extra virgin olive oil**
salt
120g **watercress**

SERVES 4

CONTALDO

INSALATA DI FAVE CON PESTO DI NOCI
Broad Bean Salad with Walnut Pesto

Fresh broad beans are a favourite in Italy during early summer and used to be much enjoyed by Puglian farmers, who would take some cheese and bread from home with them into the fields to eat with the beans. Even now, when the first broad beans appear, it is quite common for Italians to eat them raw and fresh. This simple salad makes a lovely side dish or starter and is a must during the season, but can also be made with frozen beans.

Blanch the broad beans in a large pan of boiling water for 5 minutes, then drain well, rinse in cold water and leave to cool. Peel off the skins and set aside.

Meanwhile, place the walnuts, garlic, chilli, olive oil and a little salt in a food processor and whiz until you obtain a thick paste.

Arrange the watercress in a serving dish together with the warm broad beans. Pour over the sauce, mix together well and serve.

120ml **extra virgin olive oil**
4 tbsp **balsamic vinegar**
1 **garlic clove**, finely chopped
a handful of **mint**, finely chopped
4 small **courgettes**
a few handfuls of **rocket leaves**

SERVES 4

CONTALDO

INSALATA DI ZUCCHINE CON MENTA E RUCOLA
Courgette Salad with Fresh Mint and Rocket

It was the end of spring while we were on the Amalfi coast shooting the first programme for the series, and courgettes were plentiful. As it was so hot, I decided to use them raw in a salad. When sliced very thinly, courgettes are delicious raw and marry extremely well with fresh mint. The longer you leave the courgettes to marinate before serving, the better this salad becomes.

Whisk the olive oil and vinegar together with the garlic and mint in a small bowl, and set aside. Trim the ends of the courgettes and, with a potato peeler or mandolin, slice them lengthways into wafer-thin slices. Add the courgette slices to the dressing, mix well and leave to marinate for 10 minutes, or more.

Place the marinated courgette slices on a platter. Add the rocket leaves, toss together and serve.

350g **asparagus**
50ml aged **balsamic vinegar** or
   juice of 1 lemon
3 tbsp **extra virgin olive oil**
salt and freshly ground **black
   pepper**
80g **Parmesan**, freshly shaved

SERVES 4

PARMESAN CHEESE
Carluccio

Parmigiano Reggiano is a semi-fat hard
cow's milk cheese, which can only be
made in the provinces of Parma, Reggio
Emilia, Modena, Mantova and Bologna.
After pressing, up to 30kg wheels of
cheese are salted, then dried and aged
for up to 20 months in high-ceilinged
rooms. The wheels are turned every
few days to allow the internal salt to be
distributed equally.

Grana Padano is a similar cheese made
out of the above designated areas, usually
north of the River Po. It is often aged
for less time and is much cheaper than
Parmesan, although both cheeses have
official denominations.

Parmesan or Grana Padano should be
bought in chunks, and grated fresh on
foods such as pasta and risotto. They also
both make for good eating cheeses too.

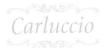

INSALATA DI ASPARAGI CRUDI CON PARMIGIANO
Raw Asparagus Salad with Parmesan

*Eating vegetables raw is a modern development in Italy, and it is
becoming more popular. In many restaurants you see dishes named
'carpaccio' of this or that. I don't like this much, as carpaccio, for
me, is so much associated with beef, but I am certainly not against
eating some vegetables raw. This is a useful dish for accompanying
fish or meat, or served as an antipasti. Like the courgette, asparagus
is a very seasonal vegetable and in Italy they truly do eat it only
during its short early summer season. One local variety is the
famous asparagus of Bassano, which is white – because it has been
earthed up, never seeing the light of day – and is extremely tender.*

Cut off the asparagus tips and set aside. Trim the remaining stems,
peeling and discarding all the stringy parts. Cut the trimmed stems
into fine julienne matchsticks, and arrange, with the whole tips,
on a platter.

Dress with vinegar or lemon juice, olive oil and salt and pepper to
taste. Sprinkle the Parmesan shavings on top and serve.

FRUTTA E DOLCI
FRUIT AND
DESSERTS

A MEAL IN ITALY USUALLY ENDS WITH SEASONAL FRUIT. A bowl of apples, pears, plums, grapes or kaki (persimmon or Sharon fruit) might be offered in the autumn, or watermelon, cherries, apricots or peaches in the summer. The Italians do not finish a meal with cheese, as the French do, but they might have some before the fruit – a chunk of Taleggio or Fontina – and might even have it with the fruit (Gorgonzola with pears is good, for instance). Sometimes a *macedonia di frutta* (fruit salad) is made, usually dressed with some freshly squeezed lemon or orange juice and sprinkled with sugar. In winter, the fruit might be baked or stewed, and made into *crostate di frutta* (fruit tarts) and, in the north (with its Germanic influences), enclosed in dumplings or strüdels. Gluts of fruit have always been turned into compotes and jams.

CONTALDO

I remember ricotta cheese, sweetened with a little sugar, being one of the few desserts we would have at home. It was such a treat, probably because the ricotta was freshly made by local farmers.

In one way or another, fruits are always present in Italian meals, leaving little space for desserts based on pastry and creams. However, this is not to say that the Italians don't enjoy sweet and creamy puddings and cakes. We do, but these tend to be saved for special occasions such as Sundays, name days, birthdays, christenings or weddings (and perhaps once a week or so if there are children in the family!). Think of *pannacotta*, *zabaglione*, *tiramisù* and the ricotta cheese-based desserts of southern Italy (the Sicilian *cannoli* and *cassata*, for instance).

Dolci tend to be more in the form of cakes or little biscuits than the sticky puddings of elsewhere in Europe. These are either made at home – a *pan di spagna* (sponge cake) would be baked, filled and decorated for a birthday for instance – or bought. On Sundays it is common to see people heading home for lunch armed with a parcel of tiny cakes bought from the local *pasticceria* (cake shop). And we must not forget the sweet treats that are enjoyed at Christmas, among them the famous *panettone* of Milan and *panforte* of Siena.

Italian ice-cream is famous the world over, and we Italians were responsible for its spread throughout Europe (its invention is credited variously, to the Chinese, to the Arabs, to the Sicilians). Ice-creams, sorbets and granitas are still traditionally – and enthusiastically – eaten during the evening *passeggiata* (stroll) in the summer months.

166

CONTALDO

150g **butter**, softened at room temperature, plus extra for greasing
190g **caster sugar**
3 tbsp **water**, plus extra for glazing
1 **orange**, cut into ½cm slices
3 **eggs**, beaten
200g **self-raising flour**
180g **ground almonds**
a pinch of **salt**
grated zest of ½ **orange**
2 tbsp thin-cut **orange marmalade**
thin slivers of **orange peel**, to decorate

SERVES 6-8

TORTA ALL'ARANCIA CARAMELIZATA
Caramelised Orange Cake

This is a much-loved family cake my sister Adriana makes, often for her sons' birthdays or when we have one of our family get-togethers. The recipe has been handed down from our nonna, who used to make it with lemons. When living in the UK in the 1980s, Adriana made the recipe with oranges instead, as British lemons were not the same as our Amalfi ones. Good-quality organic, unwaxed lemons can be substituted if you prefer, while peaches (in season) could also be used.

Preheat the oven to 180°C/Gas 4. Lightly grease an 18cm round cake tin with butter and line with greaseproof paper.

To make the caramel, dissolve half the sugar in the water in a small pan over a medium heat, then increase the heat to a boil. Wait a few minutes and, as soon as it changes to a caramel colour, remove from the heat and stir in 20g of the butter. Immediately pour the mixture into the prepared cake tin, ensuring it lines the bottom evenly. Arrange the orange slices evenly over the sugar mixture and set aside.

In a bowl, whisk together the remaining butter and sugar until creamy, add the eggs, flour, ground almonds, salt and orange zest. Pour the mixture into the tin. Bake in the oven for 50 minutes: to check if it is cooked, insert a wooden skewer, if it comes out clean, the cake is ready. Remove from the oven, leave to rest for 5 minutes, then remove from the tin and place on a flat plate with the orange slices on top.

Heat the orange marmalade in a small saucepan with a little water, then brush over the top of the cake as a glaze. Decorate with the orange peel and serve.

800g ripe **white-fleshed peaches**
  (or nectarines)
500ml **red wine**
150g **caster sugar**

SERVES 4

Carluccio

WINE *Carluccio*

Italy is one of the world's largest producers of wine, with more than 300 classified and protected wines produced from over 1,000 grape varieties. Most Italian wine is exported, although the Italians drink a lot themselves (often wines made from a small plot of grapes and kept in the cellar).

As with food, Italian wines differ from region to region, with the length of the country meaning that grapes can be grown from the snow-clad Alps right down to the almost sub-tropical south.

Many of the most prestigious classified wines come from the north, among them Nebbiolo, Barolo and Barbaresco, as well as the sweet Moscatos. Tuscany produces some superb wines, as does the south, among them Frascati, Cannonau (Sardinia) and the Marsala of Sicily.

PESCHE UBRIACHE
Fresh White Peaches in Red Wine

When I was in a restaurant in France once, my guests were drinking a very good claret. I saw some attractive peaches on a board nearby and ended up chopping some of them into a glass, adding a little sugar, and some of the wine, to create this simple, delicious dessert. I thought I was being very creative, but learnt later that the French do it all the time! This dessert is so easy to prepare, but you must have white peaches (they can be found occasionally), and the wine must be strong (something like an Amarone).

Peel the peaches, then cut them in half and remove the stones. Cut the flesh into small chunks and place in a bowl. Pour over the wine and sugar, mix and leave to chill in the fridge for a couple of hours, for the flavours to combine.

Serve this extremely enjoyable seasonal treat either on its own or with a dollop of double cream.

CONTALDO

1 large **apple**, cored and sliced into rounds
200g **strawberries**, hulled and sliced in half
40g **walnuts**, roughly chopped
a few **celery leaves**
2 tbsp **extra virgin olive oil**
salt and freshly ground **black pepper**
100g **Gorgonzola** or dolcelatte

SERVES 4

MELE ANNURCHE CON FRAGOLE E FORMAGGIO
Apples and Strawberries with Cheese

A little fruit and cheese has always been the perfect ending to a meal. I love mele annurche, *the sweet, crunchy apples grown in the Campania region, and regarded as the best apples in southern Italy. You may be lucky to find them in a specialist market or greengrocer, but a good substitute is Pink Lady. The combination of crisp apple, sweet strawberries, tender celery leaves and creamy Gorgonzola cheese makes this a delicious, healthy choice of 'dessert'. Dolcelatte or any other semi-creamy cheese can be substituted for the Gorgonzola if you prefer.*

Combine the apple slices, strawberries, walnuts, celery leaves, olive oil and a little salt and pepper in a bowl and leave for a couple of minutes for the flavours to mingle.

Arrange the mixture on a plate with the cheese and serve.

ITALIAN CHEESES
Carluccio

Italy produces probably a great selection of cheeses, the biggest variety being found in the regions of northern Italy, where the endless and lush pastures of the pre-Alps feed animals which produce thousands of gallons of rich milk.

Soft, semi-hard and hard cheeses are produced mostly by individual farmers, but cheese is also big business in Italy, with national as well as international distribution. Toma, Fontina, Taleggio, Asiago, Gorgonzola (and dolcelatte), Castelmagno, Robiola, mascarpone, provolone and Caciocavallo are mostly produced in the north, while in the south you will find mozzarella (see page 19) and the sheep's milk pecorino (Romano and Sardo).

Many Italian cheeses have official denominations, and all are eaten raw or used in cooking.

Carluccio

APFELSTRUDEL
Tyrolean Apple Pastry

This dish is usually associated with Germany and Austria, but in the regions of Italy that border these countries various food influences (such as speck, sauerkraut *and* goulash*) have crossed national boundaries. Although the classic* strüdel *is made with apples, it can be made with various fillings – such as cherries, apricots, or even peaches – and can be eaten warm or cold, as a pudding, or served at tea-time. You could make a* strüdel *dough from scratch, but it is fiddly and time-consuming. It's much easier just to use filo pastry, which you can buy anywhere.*

For the filling, put the apples in a pan with the butter, water and sugar, and cook together for 8–10 minutes, until the apples have softened slightly, but still retain their shape. Remove from the heat, add the cinnamon, raisins and juice and the breadcrumbs and stir to combine – the breadcrumbs will bind everything together. Leave to cool.

Preheat the oven to 180°C/Gas 4.

Brush a suitably sized baking tray with a little of the melted butter. Spread out one sheet of filo on the baking tray, and brush with some more of the butter. Repeat the process with all four sheets, placing them on top of each other, brushing with melted butter each time. Spoon the apple mixture along the middle of the pastry and roll up – from the bottom first, then the sides, ending with the top – to make into a parcel, seam-side down. (If you like, you can even scrunch up some extra filo pastry to make a decoration for the top.)

Brush all over with the remaining butter and bake in the oven for 15–20 minutes, or until the top is crisp and golden. Check after 10 minutes; if it is browning too quickly, reduce the heat a little. Dust with icing sugar and serve with double cream.

50g **unsalted butter**, melted
4 sheets **filo pastry**, 32 x 37cm, about 150g
icing sugar, for dusting

APPLE FILLING
800g **cooking apples**, peeled, cored and cut into small chunks
50g **unsalted butter**
100ml **water**
100g **caster sugar**
1 tsp **ground cinnamon**
3 tbsp soft **raisins**, soaked in the juice and finely grated zest of 1 large orange
a large handful of fresh **breadcrumbs**

SERVES 4

1 x 400g packet ready-made **puff pastry**
plain flour, for dusting
finely grated zest of 1 **lemon**

FILLING
300g **ricotta**
200g **mascarpone cheese**
200g **candied peel** (citron and orange preferably, roughly chopped
120g **caster sugar**
6 **eggs**, separated

SERVES 8

TORTA DI RICOTTA E LIMONE
Ricotta and Lemon Tart

This is a delicious, inter-regional lemon tart – made with fresh ricotta cheese, typical of the south, and a little mascarpone, a cream cheese of the north. Try to get sheep's milk ricotta if you can as it is much tastier. When we filmed the making of this tart, I served it with pears in red wine. To make them, tuck eight pears into a suitably sized dish with high sides and bake in the same temperature oven for half an hour until the skins start to bubble. Pour over enough good red wine to cover, sprinkle with caster sugar and bake for another half an hour, by which time the wine will have reduced to a sweet syrup.

Preheat the oven to 180°C/Gas 4.

Roll out the pastry on a lightly floured work surface until it is 2–3mm thick. Lay over a 25cm loose-bottomed tart tin, and gently push the pastry into the base and up and over the sides. There will quite a bit of overhang. Cover with a damp cloth while you make the filling.

In a large bowl, mix the ricotta, mascarpone and candied peel with 100g of the sugar and five of the egg yolks.

Put all six egg whites in another large, clean bowl and whisk until fluffy. Add the remaining sugar and continue whisking until stiff. Using a large metal spoon, fold the whites through the ricotta mixture, then pour into the pastry-lined tart tin. Fold in the overhanging pastry and brush with the reserved beaten egg yolk. Bake in the preheated oven for 30 minutes, until the pastry is risen and golden and the filling retains a slight wobble.

Leave to cool for 2 hours, then sprinkle with lemon zest. Serve either on its own or with roasted pears in red wine (see above).

CONTALDO

PAN DI SPAGNA
Italian Sponge Cake

It is said that this sponge was first made by a Genoese chef during a visit to Spain at a banquet for the Genoese ambassador in the 1700s. It was then known as pâte genoise, *later becoming* pan di spagna, *and is now very popular across Italy. You can fill it with* crema pasticcera *(custard cream), jam, Nutella, ricotta, whatever you like, drizzle it with water and liqueur to make it more moist, or simply eat it plain. Here I have given you the basic sponge recipe and a syrup for soaking it in; the filling I leave to you.*

Preheat the oven to 180°C/Gas 4. Lightly grease a 25cm round cake tin with butter and line with greaseproof paper.

Sift the flours, salt and baking powder into a bowl and set aside. Whisk the egg yolks and icing sugar together until light and fluffy. In a separate bowl, whisk the egg whites until stiff. Gradually fold the flours, egg whites and lemon zest into the egg yolk mixture until well combined. Pour the mixture into the prepared cake tin and bake in the oven for 35 minutes, until risen and golden. Do not to open the oven door during cooking as this will make the cake sink. Leave the cake to cool, then remove from the tin and cut horizontally into two layers.

Place the syrup ingredients in a small pan and cook over a medium heat, stirring, until the sugar has dissolved, the liquid has reduced a little and the flavours have infused. Remove from the heat and leave to cool. Discard the citrus rinds, then drizzle the syrup over the sponge halves. Leave to soak into the sponge for at least one hour, overnight if possible.

When the sponge is ready, sandwich together with your chosen filling. Dust all over with lots of icing sugar and serve.

butter, for greasing
85g **plain flour**
75g **cornflour**
a pinch of **salt**
1 tsp **baking powder**
6 **eggs**, separated
180g **icing sugar**, plus extra for dusting
grated zest of ½ **lemon**

SYRUP
350ml **water**
80ml **strega** or rum
2 tbsp **caster sugar**
3 slices of **orange rind**
3 slices of **lemon rind**

SERVES 8

½ litre **water**
300g **sugar**
½ litre **lemon juice**
   (about 6–8 large lemons)
grated zest of 1 **lemon**

SERVES 4

CONTALDO

GRANITA DI LIMONE
Lemon Granita

On the Amalfi coast, where the famous Sfusato lemon grows, this thirst-quenching slush is a most refreshing and welcoming treat on a hot day, sold in bars and ice-cream parlours. If you can find Amalfi lemons then please use them, otherwise go for large, unwaxed organic lemons. You can also substitute the lemons for oranges, if you prefer.

Place the water and sugar in a small pan and gently simmer over a low heat for 10 minutes, until the sugar dissolves and the liquid reduces slightly and develops a syrup-like consistency. Remove from the heat and leave to cool.

Strain the lemon juice through a fine sieve and add to the cooled syrup. Mix well and leave to rest for 30 minutes, stirring from time to time.

Stir in the lemon zest, pour into a plastic container with a lid and place in the freezer. After 30 minutes, remove and beat with a fork, then place back in the freezer for another 30 minutes. Repeat the procedure three times, for a total of 4 hours. Keep in the freezer until ready to use. Alternatively, place in an ice-cream maker and churn until it is well amalgamated, but not as firm as ice-cream.

Divide between 4 glasses and serve.

6 **egg yolks**
150g **caster sugar**
120ml **Marsala**, Vin Santo,
  Moscato or any sweet wine

TO SERVE (OPTIONAL)
8 **amaretti biscuits** or small
  meringues
320g **raspberries** (or wild
  strawberries)
4 **strawberries**, hulled and halved

SERVES 4

Carluccio

ZABAGLIONE
Foamed Egg and Sugar

The origins of this flavourful dessert are hotly disputed: is it from Florence, Piedmont or Sicily; is it new or is it old? The one thing that is not in dispute is that the mixture originated in Italy – influencing the French sabayon – that it has been used over the years (possibly without the alcohol) as a food for children and invalids, and that it is closely associated with love and seduction. Zabaglione can be served warm, straight from the pot, but is good cold as well. I like it in a glass, served with some fruit and some amaretti biscuits or small meringues.

Put the egg yolks and sugar in a round-bottomed bowl and whisk for a few minutes to obtain a whitish foam. Stand the bowl over a pan of gently simmering water over a low heat. Add the Marsala, and continue beating, still over a gentle heat, until the mixture thickens to a foam.

You now have a choice. Either pour the zabaglione into four glasses and serve warm, with whichever biscuits you desire. Alternatively, you can spread the raspberries over four plates, pour over the zabaglione and decorate with the halved strawberries.

CONTALDO

500ml **milk**
15g **plain flour**
30g **caster sugar**
1 **vanilla pod**, halved lengthways
  and seeds removed
80ml **Amaretto liqueur**
100g **dark chocolate**, finely
  chopped
50g **unsalted butter**
30g **amaretti biscuits**, crushed

SERVES 6

BUDINO AL CIOCCOLATO E AMARETTO
Chocolate and Amaretto Pudding

A simple, old-fashioned chocolate pudding, which can be served either warm or chilled and is very easy to prepare. The addition of Amaretto liqueur gives it a bit of a kick but not too much. A perfect dessert to serve when you are in the mood for a little romance!

Put the milk in a saucepan and warm over a low heat.

Combine the flour, sugar and vanilla seeds in a medium-sized saucepan, add a little of the milk and whisk to a smooth paste. Add the remainder of the milk and warm over a low heat, whisking all the while to prevent lumps from forming. Stir in the Amaretto liqueur and continue to whisk until the mixture has begun to thicken. Remove from the heat, add the chocolate and butter and stir to combine.

Spoon the mixture into serving glasses and serve either warm or cold, topped with the crushed amaretti biscuits.

1kg **ricotta**
140g **caster sugar**
70g **candied fruit**, finely chopped
40g **flaked almonds**
50g **chocolate chips**
1 tbsp **cocoa powder**, plus extra
for dusting
600g **panettone**, cut into
2 round discs and the
rest lengthways into slices
lengthways 2.5cm thick
175ml **Vin Santo**

SERVES 6

CONTALDO

ZUCCOTTO DI PANETTONE
Panettone and Ricotta Pudding

Panettone *originated in the early 1900s and was made by poor people at Christmas time with leftover bread dough and whatever dried fruit they could find. After World War I, the confectionery companies Motta and Alemagna copied the idea, and the cake achieved worldwide fame. Zuccotto, a traditional northern Italian dessert, is usually made with plain sponge, but during the festive season it is a wonderful way for using up leftover* panettone.

Mix together half of the ricotta with half of the sugar in a medium-sized bowl until creamy. Then fold in half of the candied fruit, half of the almonds and half of the chocolate chips until well combined, and set aside. In another medium-sized bowl, mix the remaining ricotta and sugar with the cocoa powder until creamy. Stir in the remaining candied fruit, flaked almonds and chocolate chips and set aside.

Line a 15cm diameter pudding basin or a deep bowl with clingfilm, leaving quite a bit of excess around the edges. Line with the slices of *panettone* and, using a pastry brush, brush about three-quarters of the Vin Santo over the cake slices. Fill with the chocolate ricotta mixture, which should fill half the basin. Take one of the round *panettone* discs, place over the top and press, then drizzle over some of the Vin Santo. Fill with the white ricotta mixture and cover with the other *panettone* disc, then drizzle with the remaining Vin Santo. Bring up the overhang of clingfilm and place a weight on top (a plate with a bag of sugar on it, for example), and place in the fridge for at least 6 hours.

Remove from the fridge, take off the weight and the clingfilm over the top. Turn upside-down on a plate. Carefully remove the pudding basin and peel off the clingfilm. Dust with sifted cocoa powder and serve.

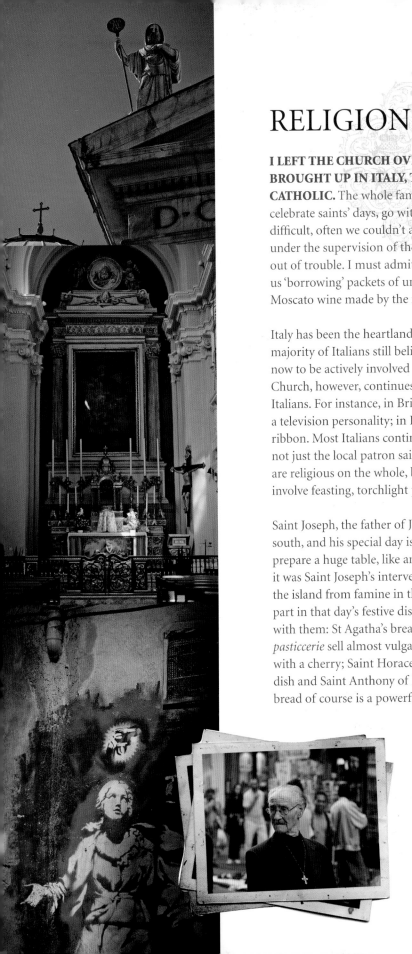

RELIGION

I LEFT THE CHURCH OVER 40 YEARS AGO. HOWEVER, I WAS BROUGHT UP IN ITALY, THEREFORE I WAS BROUGHT UP A CATHOLIC. The whole family would go to mass, to confession, would celebrate saints' days, go without meat when proscribed (that was not difficult, often we couldn't afford it), and eat fish on Fridays. And growing up under the supervision of the local priest was good for us children, as it kept us out of trouble. I must admit, though, that our priestly chaperonage didn't stop us 'borrowing' packets of unblessed wafers from the sacristy, and tasting the Moscato wine made by the nuns...

Italy has been the heartland of Catholicism since the fourth century. A majority of Italians still believe in God, although less than 50 per cent are said now to be actively involved with the Church, and attendance is declining. The Church, however, continues to play a substantial role in the lives of ordinary Italians. For instance, in Britain, an inauguration might be done by a royal or a television personality; in Italy a representative of the Church always cuts the ribbon. Most Italians continue to celebrate the annual feast days of saints, and not just the local patron saint of a city, town or village. Most of these fiestas are religious on the whole, but some are increasingly secular, and all of them involve feasting, torchlight processions, special masses and firework displays.

Saint Joseph, the father of Jesus, for instance, is particularly revered in the south, and his special day is 19th March, also the Italian Father's Day. Families prepare a huge table, like an altar, groaning with breads and pastries. In Sicily, it was Saint Joseph's intervention – with the *fava* or broad bean – that saved the island from famine in the Middle Ages. As a result, the bean plays a major part in that day's festive dishes. Most saints have a particular food associated with them: St Agatha's breasts were cut off, for instance, and local Sicilian *pasticcerie* sell almost vulgar hemispherical cakes, iced in white, and topped with a cherry; Saint Horace of Lecce in Puglia gives his name to an aubergine dish and Saint Anthony of Padua has a bread – as do many other saints, for bread of course is a powerful Christian symbol, particularly in Italy.

Italians also celebrate the more familiar Christian festivals, in fact we like to celebrate anything! Christmas and Easter are huge in religious terms, but also in terms of food tradition. On Christmas Eve, the Romans eat *capitone* (a large grilled eel), and everyone enjoys *panettone*, the light yeasted cake now so familiar worldwide. At Easter, a dove-shaped version of *panettone* is eaten (*la paloma*), as well as lamb or kid dishes, eggs and

wheat (the meat representing Christ, the egg life, and the wheat resurrection). The Ligurians make a *torta pasqualina* (a vegetable and ricotta pie with a pastry layer for each year of Christ's life), and the Neapolitans bake a ricotta cake called *pastiera napoletana*. On All Souls' Day, 2nd November, special breads, cakes and biscuits are made, while at the start of Lent, we Italians have pancakes and many delicious recipes evolved to replace the forbidden meat, such as Gennaro's *Polpette di Melanzane* (see page 95).

Weddings and christenings still take place in church, and both offer another opportunity for Italian feasting. Italian brides have a satin purse (*la borsa*) attached to their dresses, in which guests put money (perhaps to help pay for all the food!). It is considered bad luck to purchase the pastries for an Italian christening, so everything is home-made. And after both occasions, guests are offered a little bag containing sugared almonds, known as 'confetti'.

Roman Catholicism may be the major religion of Italy, but there are also mature Protestant and Jewish communities. Jews have lived in Italy since Roman times, and inevitably their culinary thinking has had an influence: at one point in the Roman ghetto, Jews were *friggitori*, deep-fryers of foods sold on the street, and familiar dishes such as *carciofi alla giudia* (fried globe artichokes) and *fritelle di baccalà* (salt cod fritters) are direct echoes of this. There is also a growing Muslim community in Italy and increasingly, despite opposition (although Islam has come to be the second largest faith in Italy, it is not formally recognised by the Government) Islamic culinary thinking is having an impact. Indeed, I read that after the foot and mouth threat some years ago, Islamic halal butchers were even providing Florentine restaurants with T-bone steaks for the famous *bistecca fiorentina*!

Carluccio

300ml **water**
½ glass **white wine**
280g **plain flour**
vegetable oil, for frying
preserved **morello cherries**
icing sugar, sifted

CREMA PASTICCERA
4 **egg yolks**
100g **sugar**
30g **cornflour**
375ml **milk**
½ **vanilla pod**

MAKES ABOUT 20

CONTALDO

ZEPPOLE DI SAN GIUSEPPE
Doughnuts

Created in Naples in the 19th century, zeppole are traditionally eaten throughout Italy to celebrate the feast day of Saint Joseph on 19th March. The doughnuts are known by various names in different regions: sfinci, fritelle *and* bigne *among others, and can be eaten plain with just a little sugar sprinkled over the top, drizzled with honey, filled with cream or even with anchovies as they do in Calabria.*

To make the *crema pasticcera*, whisk the egg yolks and the sugar in a bowl until light and fluffy. Add the cornflour and continue to whisk. Pour the milk into a saucepan together with the vanilla pod and bring gently to the boil. As it begins to boil, remove from the heat and beat in the egg mixture. Return to a medium heat and cook, stirring with a wooden spoon, until it begins to boil again. Remove from the heat, pour into a container and leave to cool, stirring from time to time.

For the *zeppole*, pour the water and wine into a medium-sized pan and bring to the boil. Remove from the heat, add the flour and whisk together well, making sure there are no lumps. Return to the heat and cook for a further minute, stirring, until the mixture comes away from the sides of the pan and you obtain a soft dough. Leave to cool.

Spread a little oil on a clean work surface or board and gently knead the dough for a couple of minutes. Roll the dough into a large sausage and cut into slices about 2cm thick. Roll out each slice into a sausage about 15–17cm in length and form them into hoops. Heat enough oil to half fill a medium-sized saucepan, drop the doughnuts in and cook until golden, about 3 minutes. Remove and shake off the excess oil.

Spoon the *crema pasticcera* into a piping bag and pipe a rosette around the centre of the *zeppole*. Top with a cherry and sprinkle with icing sugar.

Carluccio

500g **dried figs**, roughly chopped
500g **dried apricots**, finely diced
200g **shelled hazelnuts**, toasted
150g **candied lemon peel** (cedro
   lemon, preferably), diced
125g **candied orange peel**, diced
1 tbsp freshly ground **black
   pepper**
a few drops of **vanilla extract**

MAKES ABOUT 1.5KG

SALAME DI FICHI, ALBICOCCHE E NOCCIOLE
Fig, Dried Apricot and Hazelnut Salami

Fruit is normally eaten fresh in Italy when in season, but gluts are preserved in some way, by making into jam, by preserving the fruits whole in syrup, or by drying. Many sweet things are saved for special occasions, and this idea, from Le Marche, is popular at Christmas. It is fun and easy to prepare, and keeps for a long time: if you want to upgrade it a little, try adding some chopped pistachio nuts to the mixture.

Put the fig pieces in a food processor and blend until you have a sticky paste. Transfer to a bowl along with all the other ingredients, and mix together well.

Divide the mixture in half and spoon each portion along the middle of a sheet of rice paper. Roll up tightly in the paper, shaping each into a 'salami' about 30cm in length, and 6cm thick, then roll the rice paper 'salami' up tightly in a piece of greaseproof paper. Tie with string. Store in a cool, dry place for about a couple of days before eating.

Remove the greaseproof paper and serve cut into thin slices, with coffee, dessert wine or cheese. The 'salami' will keep for a month or so.

MERENDE
SNACKS

MERENDE MEANS 'SNACKS', AND THE WORD CAN APPLY TO FOODS EATEN BETWEEN MEALS, TO FOODS TAKEN ON PICNICS, AND TO THE LIGHT MEAL (A 'TEA' IN ENGLISH) SERVED TO CHILDREN WHEN THEY COME HOME STARVING FROM SCHOOL.

Although we usually think of Italy as a country where people traditionally eat at home, three times a day, surrounded by their families, *merende* are part of everyday life. While Italy hasn't traditionally had a snack culture, things have changed and with the modern pace of life, people might not have the time to have a proper breakfast before travelling to the office or to go home for lunch as they once did. Whether it's a morning brioche grabbed from the *pasticceria* (cake shop), or a lunch-time, late-afternoon or early panini or wedge of pizza bought from a deli, food shop or stall, it is undoubtedly true these days that most Italian people will at some point in the day enjoy a snack of some sort.

Carluccio
Years ago, in Borgofranco, there was an avalanche, and huge blocks of granite piled up at the bottom of the hill. These formed natural caves which now belong to the workers of the town, and because the caves are cool and aerated, wine, cheese and salami are stored there. Occasionally, on going to check the condition of their stores, the cave-owners take with them some bread, tomatoes, fruit and wine. Sometimes they bring along friends, some meat and a barbecue, and there is great merriment. That's what I call a merenda.

Most of these *merende* will be bought at specialist street stalls, from pastry shops, or from the *rosticceria* (a type of coffee-shop/restaurant/deli found in all towns and cities in Italy). The word *rosticceria* refers to roasting on a spit, and indeed you can find whole chicken and joints of game here, as well as sausages, a variety of salads, *arancini* (fried risotto balls), mini-pizzas and a huge variety of delicious little nibbles, which all vary from region to region.

The most traditional *merenda*, though, is the light meal given to ravenous girls and boys when they return home from school. This is usually served around 4–5 o'clock, well after the midday lunch, and before dinner which is usually between 7 and 8 o'clock. A typical *merenda* would consist of some bread and jam, with a glass of milk or cup of hot chocolate, or a *salami panino* or a slice of cake, whatever the mother has at home which is fairly quick to prepare and will be nutritiously satisfying until dinner time.

TRECCIA DI PATATE, FAVE E SALAME
Country Plait Bread with Potato, Broad Beans and Salami

200g **potatoes**, peeled
450g **fresh or frozen broad beans**
3 tbsp **extra virgin olive oil**, plus
  extra for oiling
1 **garlic clove**, left whole
salt and freshly ground **black
  pepper**
100g **salami**, cut into small cubes
500g **strong white flour**, plus
  extra for dusting
15g **fresh yeast**, dissolved in a
  little lukewarm water,
  or 1 x 10g sachet of dried yeast
  (see packet for instructions)
200ml **lukewarm water**, plus an
  additional 3 tbsp for brushing

SERVES 6–8

*This is a typical country bread from Puglia, traditionally made
by farmers' housewives with all sorts of leftovers to provide a
substantial meal for the farmer while working in the fields.*

Add the potatoes to a pan of lightly salted water, bring to the boil and
simmer until tender. Drain, mash and leave to cool. Remove the skins
from the broad beans (if you are using frozen beans you will need to
blanch them for a few minutes in boiling salted water beforehand).
Heat two tablespoons of the olive oil in a pan, add the garlic clove
and sauté for a minute, then add the broad beans, season to taste and
cook for a few minutes. Lower the heat, cover and cook for a further 5
minutes. Discard the garlic clove and place in a bowl. Add the salami,
mix well and leave to cool.

Place the flour onto a clean work surface or into a large bowl, make
a well in the centre and add the dissolved yeast, potato, broad bean
mixture and water. Mix together well until you obtain a smooth
dough. Form into a ball, cover with a cloth and leave in a warm place
to rise for 1 hour, until the dough has doubled in size.

On a lightly floured work surface, divide the dough into three portions.
Roll out each into a long thin sausage, roughly 60cm in length. When
you have all three ready, shape into a plait, place on a lightly oiled
baking tray, closing the edges to form a round bread. Cover with a cloth
and leave in a warm place to rise for a further 30 minutes.

Preheat the oven to 220°C/Gas 7. Combine the water and the
remaining olive oil and brush the top of the bread. Place in the oven,
lower the temperature to 200°C/Gas 6 and bake for about 40 minutes,
until golden-brown. Remove from the oven and leave to cool.

400g **plain flour**
a pinch of **salt**
1 x 10g sachet of **dried yeast**
 (see packet for instructions)
40g **lard**, roughly cut into small
 pieces
225ml **water**

FILLING
16 slices of **Parma ham**
250g *stracchino* **cheese** (available
 in good delicatessens)
a bunch of **rocket leaves**

SERVES 8

CONTALDO

PIADINA
Filled Emilian Flatbread

'Nothing speaks more of Romagna than this bread of ours – it is a symbol that speaks of devotion to our land.' Giovanni Pascoli

This old recipe for thin flatbread is so traditional in Emilia-Romagna that even the poet, Pascoli, wrote about it. It is now a popular snack throughout Italy – sold in specialised kiosks called piadinerie *and filled with cured meats, cheese and vegetables. They are best filled while still hot from the pan, when the prosciutto and cheese melt inside, and eaten immediately. The original recipe uses* strutto *(lard) – if you prefer, you can use butter, although I do think lard gives a nicer flavour.*

Place the flour, salt and yeast on a clean work surface or in a large bowl. Make a well in the centre and add the lard. Gradually pour in the water and mix with your hands until you obtain a smooth dough. Shape into a ball and knead for 5 minutes. Leave to rise in a warm place for 30 minutes, or until about doubled in size.

Knead the dough for a couple of minutes, then divide into eight portions. Roll each portion out into circles approximately 1mm thick. Heat a large frying pan, add one of the dough portions and cook for 2 minutes on each side. Remove and cover with the Parma ham, cheese and rocket, then fold in half. Serve.

ALTRE MERENDE DI PANE
Other Bread-based Snacks

The following are simple ideas, rather than formal recipes, based on that beloved staple of Italian food, bread – something the Italians eat an incredible amount of with everything…

BURRO E ACCIUGHE (BUTTER AND ANCHOVIES)

Take some sliced country bread (preferably Puglian), and some very good unsalted butter (preferably Alpine). Spread the bread with the butter, then top with some anchovies drained of their oil. Eat.

In Piedmont, they mix their anchovies with a green sauce to create *acciughe in salsa verde*. To make this, take some dough from the middle of a slice of bread, soak it in some white wine vinegar for a couple of minutes and then squeeze dry. Whiz this bread in a blender or food processor to make crumbs. Mix a handful of finely chopped parsley with a finely chopped garlic clove and a little dried chilli, add the breadcrumbs, then stir in enough oil to make a thick sauce. Put the drained anchovies in a dish and spread the sauce over them. Serve on buttered bread.

SALAME E FORMAGGIO (SALAMI AND CHEESE)

An arrangement of various types of Italian meats and cheeses on a platter, this offering would work as an antipasti plate. The meats could include *mortadella*, *salami*, *prosciutto* and *culatello*, while the cheeses could vary according to region: in the south they might include pecorino, Caciocavallo and mozzarella; in the north, Gorgonzola, Fontina, Parmesan and Castelmagno. Cut these in chunks or slices. Serve with some pickles – little gherkins, onions (those on page 156 would be good), olives, artichokes and porcini (cep). Accompany with *grissini*, *tarallucci* (see page 194), or very good fresh country bread.

BREAD CONTALDO

'The bread of life' and bread as 'the body of Christ' are phrases recited during masses in all Catholic countries. But as well as its religious connotations, bread is a major and highly respected staple in Italy. In Italian homes and restaurants, a meal would not be complete without some accompanying bread. Usually bought daily from the local *panetteria* (baker), bread types range from the highly prized *Pugliese*, to *focaccia*, *ciabatta*, *piadina*, and the harder breads such as *grissini* and *taralli*, while pizza is the classic flatbread.

Leftover bread is never wasted, and the notion that it is bad luck to put bread in the dustbin has passed down the generations. Leftover bread tends to be made into breadcrumbs, used for fillings, turned into *panzanella* (bread salad) and bread soups, or used as a base for *bruschetta* or *crostini*.

200g **semolina flour**
200g **plain flour**, plus extra for dusting
1 tsp **salt**
1 tbsp freshly ground **black pepper**
1 tbsp **fennel seeds**
1 x 7g sachet **dried yeast**, dissolved in 150ml lukewarm water
100ml **extra virgin olive oil**

MAKES 40–50

TARALLUCCI
Savoury Fennel Biscuits

There is a saying in southern Italy, where these biscuits come from, that even the most heated discussion invariably ends up peacefully, over tarallucci e vino *(biscuits and wine). The equivalent of the northern* grissini, *these biscuits are made from a dough that is boiled first, then baked. Crisp and crumbly, they make a perfect snack for hungry children back from school, especially if accompanied by some olives and cheese. Needless to say, hungry adults would enjoy them with a glass of red wine and some pecorino too…*

Place the two flours in a pile on the work surface or a large bowl, add the salt, pepper and fennel seeds and mix. Make a well in the centre, add the dissolved yeast and olive oil and mix to a soft dough. Knead it for 5 minutes, then cover and leave to rise for about 2 hours, until about doubled in size.

Knead the dough thoroughly again, about 5 minutes. Divide the dough into four and, on a lightly floured work surface, roll out each piece, using the palms of your hands, into baton shapes, 2cm in diameter. Cut each baton into 10cm lengths. Join the ends of the lengths together, and press to seal.

Preheat the oven to 180°C/Gas 4 and bring a large saucepan of lightly salted water to the boil.

Plunge the dough circles into the boiling water; you will probably have to do this in batches. After 5 minutes, or when they come to surface, scoop them out and leave to drain.

Place the biscuits on a baking sheet and bake for 10 minutes. Lower the temperature to 150°C/Gas 2 and cook for a further 15 minutes, until crisp and crumbly. Leave to cool on a wire rack.

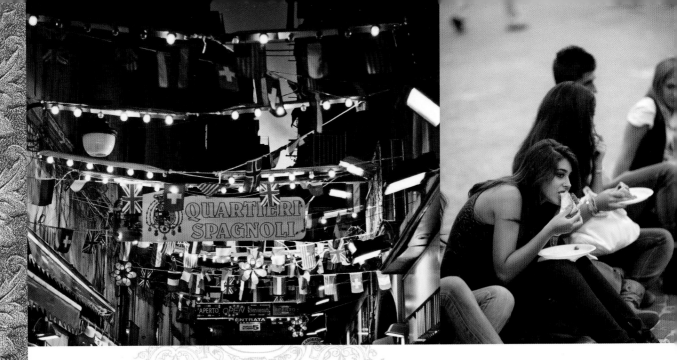

STREET FOOD AND IMMIGRATION

IN ITALY THE CONSUMPTION OF FOOD IS A RITUAL THAT LASTS FROM MORNING TO NIGHT. Much of this consumption takes place outside the home, on the streets, and most of what is eaten is snack food, or *merende*. Eating food in the street has been normal for the poor of Italy for centuries, primarily because they had no access to cooking facilities at home.

Street foods today are sold from restaurants, kiosks, market stands and stalls, and vehicles like ice-cream vans. The range of street foods consumed now in Italy is vast and, naturally, differs from region to region: in Puglia it is raw seafood; in Marche lambs' innards; in Emilia-Romagna you will find the classic *piadina* (a type of filled pancake) as well as a fried *gnocco* filled with the region's salami. In Tuscany you find *cecina*, a chickpea cake and panini

filled with *lampredotto* (tripe) in Florence, while in Rome, kiosks sell sandwiches of the famous *porchetta* (roast suckling pig). In Cagliari in Sardinia, it is traditional during the summer to consume *ricci di mare* (sea urchins) at kiosks along the seafront, before lunch. In Palermo, Sicily's capital, *pani ca' meusa* (a bread roll with veal spleen, thought to be of Jewish origin) is sold at stalls outside nightclubs in the early hours of the morning. During the day stallholders at the market sell boiled octopus, *stigghiole alle brace* (grilled innards of goat, lamb or veal), as well as *sfincione*, the Sicilian version of pizza, *panelle* (chickpea fritters), *cazzilli* (potato croquettes) and *arancini* (risotto balls).

But the most renowned Italian street food of all must be pizza. Worldwide, flatbreads have always been a basic food of the poor, and at first the Italian version, pizza, was simply a bread dough made with lard – filling, portable and cheap, and despised elsewhere. But in Naples it gradually acquired toppings, principally tomato (after the fruit became popular only a couple of centuries ago). It is amazing how this humble Neapolitan food has become so famous, and how many different types there are now.

Memories of street food in my home village of Minori are very vivid. My friends and I actually became sellers of street food, collecting prickly pears in the summer to hawk along the seafront! There were also small stands selling snails cooked with garlic, chilli and parsley, wrapped in paper. During the winter, stalls sold roasted chestnuts, *sofritto*, a mixture of offal, served on hunks of good country bread, and at Christmas and on feast days there were *zeppole* (doughnuts, see page 186). Although the street foods of my childhood still exist today, there are definite changes taking place in Italy, especially in the larger towns and cities. The globalisation of eating habits and the proliferation of fast-food chains are beginning to threaten traditional street food. There are pockets of resistance, however: in the small town of Altamura in Puglia, a McDonald's was forced to close in favour of a traditional bakery!

Immigration too is having an effect on Italy's food culture and traditions in general. From being a country of mass emigration, Italy has over the last 20 years received many immigrants, with some 7.5 per cent of the population now coming from abroad, and these immigrants are having an effect on the food. Turkish and Middle Eastern kebab houses are appearing in cities like Milan and Rome, as well as Chinese and Indian restaurants. Even sushi is on offer! For younger Italians this type of food is a novelty and a welcome addition to the foods of their childhood. For the older generation, it is a different story and the majority would not dare try anything new such as a kebab. Unfamiliar ingredients are also appearing in Italian markets, such as ginger, and traditional recipes are subtly changing as they are incorporated.

Italians are very conscious of these changes and there are movements which are desperately trying to protect the future of traditional street foods. Books have been written, as have countless newspaper and magazine articles. A cultural association, Streetfood, has been set up to promote awareness of traditional foods, and organises events throughout Italy such as the International Street Food Festival in Cesena. After all, street food is indelibly linked to the history and traditions of the country, the diverse culinary culture and diverse ingredients of each region and often offers the most truly authentic flavour of a city or region.

CONTALDO

500g **strong plain flour**, plus
  extra for dusting
10g **salt**
10g **fresh yeast**
325ml lukewarm water
a few **dried breadcrumbs**
  (see page 154) for sprinkling

TOPPING
300g tinned **plum tomatoes**
salt and freshly ground **black
  pepper**
4 tablespoons **extra virgin olive
  oil**, plus extra for drizzling
25g **Parmesan**, freshly grated
a few **basil leaves** or some dried
  oregano
150g **mozzarella**, roughly
  chopped

MAKES 2 LARGE PIZZAS

PIZZA CONTALDO

The origins of the word 'pizza' are
debatable: it could come from the Latin
word *pinsa* or from the Middle Eastern
pita or *pitta* (both meaning 'flatbread').
  Early pizza consisted of a dough, made
into a flatbread, used by bakers to test the
oven temperature. Filling and portable,
it was a staple of *cucina povera*, sold in
the streets of Naples in the 18th and 19th
centuries. It gradually acquired toppings,
among them tomatoes, and became a
popular snack (although it was reviled
by many).
  In 1889 a famous Neapolitan pizza-
maker, Raffaele Esposito, made a pizza
for Queen Margherita, topping it with
the colours of the Italian flag, using
tomato, basil and mozzarella. The pizza
was a hit with the Queen and, after the
emigrations of the 1950s and 1960s, the
rest of the world! Now Italians consume
around 7 million pizzas a day.

CONTALDO

LA VERA PIZZA NAPOLETANA
The True Neapolitan Pizza

*During our trip to Italy, we visited one of the oldest pizzerias in
Naples, Sorbillo, where people queue around the block to sample
their classic* pizza margherita. *You get so many varieties of pizzas
these days, and there are so many bad versions out there, that I
know why some Italians want to make it DOC, like wine...*

Preheat the oven to 250°C/Gas 9. Put the flour and salt in a large
bowl. Dissolve the yeast in the lukewarm water and gradually add to
the flour, mixing well until you obtain a dough. If you find the dough
too sticky, just add a little more flour. Shape the dough into a ball and
leave to rest, covered with a cloth, for 5 minutes. Knead the dough for
8–10 minutes and split it in half. Knead each of the pieces for a couple
of minutes and shape into balls. Sprinkle some flour on a clean kitchen
cloth and place the dough on it, then cover with a slightly damp cloth.
Leave to rise in a warm place for 30 minutes.

Meanwhile, place the tomatoes in a bowl, crush them slightly with a
fork, season and mix well. Sprinkle some flour on a clean work surface
and spread the dough into a circle about 35–40cm in diameter, making
it as thin as a pancake (being careful not to tear it), with the border
slightly thicker. Repeat with the other dough ball. Sprinkle a few
breadcrumbs on two large baking trays and place the pizza bases
on them.

Spread a little of the tomato evenly over each base – not too much, or
the pizzas will be soggy. Drizzle with the olive oil, sprinkle over the
Parmesan, add a few basil leaves or sprinkle over some oregano and
top with pieces of mozzarella cheese. Place in the oven for 7 minutes (a
couple of minutes longer if you prefer your pizza crisp). Remove from
the oven, drizzle with some more olive oil and consume immediately.

about 250g cooked **pasta**,
flavoured with tomato
or other sauce
4 **eggs**
50g **Parmesan**, freshly grated
salt and freshly ground **black
pepper**
2 tbsp finely chopped
flat-leaf parsley (optional)
8 tbsp **extra virgin olive oil**

SERVES 4

Carluccio

FRITTATA DI MACCHERONI
Leftover Pasta Omelette

Italians love their pasta so much, they had to invent a recipe that enabled them to eat it when on the move! Imagine a Spanish tortilla with eggs and potatoes: this is the Italian equivalent, with eggs and pasta. Incorporating pasta into something like an omelette is almost the only way in which you can transport it. This frittata is traditionally eaten on Easter Monday picnics or other outings. The best pasta to use is spaghetti, which can be leftovers, although in Italy the pasta is often cooked especially for the dish.

Put the cooked pasta in a large bowl. Beat the eggs, and add to the bowl, along with the Parmesan, salt, pepper and parsley, if using. Stir to combine.

Heat the olive oil in a medium non-stick frying pan until quite hot. Pour in the pasta mixture and fry over a medium heat for about 8 minutes, until the bottom is golden-brown. Put a plate over the top of the pan and invert the omelette on to the plate, then return to the pan, uncooked side down, and cook for a further 8 minutes. Remove from the heat and cut into wedges. Serve either hot or cold, as a starter, as a snack at tea-time or part of a lunch-box or picnic.

Carluccio

CROSTATINA DI MARMELLATA
Jam-topped Pastry

200g **plain flour**, plus extra for dusting
120g **unsalted butter**, cut into cubes, plus a little extra, for greasing
1 **egg**, beaten
a pinch of **salt**
1 tbsp **caster sugar**
40ml **water**
jam (apricot, strawberry, cherry, peach or anything else you happen to have)

SERVES 4–8

There are various ways of preparing this pastry, which makes use of the various jams that Italian housewives have made during the year. This one, which I first encountered in a Milan restaurant, is the one I like best, primarily because of its simplicity: the shortcrust pastry is baked blind, often in huge sheets, then simply brushed with jam. Pieces are broken off for eating, so it is not at all refined, though you could always make it a little more sophisticated by baking it in a tart tin, for instance, spreading it with jam before baking, or perhaps decorating it with lattice strips of pastry across the top.

Put the flour in a bowl and add the butter, egg, salt and sugar. Work quickly, using your fingers, mixing the butter and egg into the flour. Add the water, and bring together to form a dough, then knead for 5 minutes. Wrap and leave to rest in the refrigerator for 30 minutes.

Preheat the oven to 180°C/Gas 4.

Roll out the pastry on a lightly floured board or piece of greaseproof paper into a rectangle of about 5mm thickness. Grease a suitably sized rectangular baking tray and line with the pastry, trimming off the excess. Bake in the oven until crisp, about 15 minutes. Leave to cool, then spread the jam thinly across the top and serve.

300g good-quality **dark chocolate**
80g **caster sugar**
500ml **milk**
4 slices of good **country bread**,
  toasted
butter
jam

SERVES 4

CONTALDO

CIOCCOLATA CALDA CON PANE, BURRO E MARMELLATA
Hot Chocolate with Bread, Butter and Jam

This is a tea-time snack tradititionally offered to children when they return home from school in Italy, and is a good way of getting them to drink milk. This type of hot chocolate is also very popular in cafés throughout Italy, especially during the cooler months when warming drinks are called for.

Break up the chocolate into small pieces.

Place the sugar and milk in a small saucepan over a medium heat and stir with a wooden spoon until the sugar has dissolved. Stir in the chocolate and cook for a further 10 minutes, stirring continuously, until the chocolate has melted and the mixture has thickened slightly but is nice and creamy.

Divide between four cups and serve immediately with slices of toasted buttered bread and jam.

INDEX

CONTALDO **THANK YOU TO** Liz Przybylski for ghostwriting and organizing. Adriana Contaldo for testing recipes. Antonio Carluccio for sharing this journey with me! Chris Terry for the wonderful photos and Danny Treacy for being Chris's efficient assistant. Anna Jones and Emily Ezekiel for styling at the photoshoots. Claire Peters for the beautiful design. Susan Fleming and Simon Davis for the editing and correcting. Jane O'Shea, Helen Lewis and everyone else at Quadrille for making this book a reality. Zoe Collins and her team from Fresh One Productions – Nicola Gooch, Danny Horan, Sheena Cameron, Vicky Ewart, Carla de Nicola, Rose Walton, Maria Laura Frullini and the crew – Danny Roher, Andy Boag, Alex Macdonald, Mike Sarah and Lee Meredith. Drivers Paola and Dionisia and Alessandro and his beautiful Alfa Romeo Giulietta. Sarah Tildesly and her wonderful team of food stylists. Debbie Catchpole, my agent, and her assistant Verity O'Brien. Jamie Oliver for making this happen!

Carluccio **SPECIAL THANKS GO TO** Special thanks go to Susan Fleming for making sense of my endless hand written notes and managing to edit both of the Two Greedy Italians so beautifully. Anna-Louise Naylor-Leyland for her endless support. Chris Terry for the sumptuous photography; Sarah Tildesly and Anna Jones for food styling. To my agent Pat White, my Publisher Quadrille and those who made the book possible: Alison Cathie, Jane O'Shea, Claire Peters, Simon Davis and Marina Asenjo. And to Zoe Collins and her team at Fresh One Productions for taking this Greedy Italian back to Italy!

THE FOLLOWING PEOPLE IN ITALY ALSO DESERVE SPECIAL THANKS
Campania Mino Porporra and his Mum Antonietta, Tomaso Mansi, Andrea Reale, Comune di Minori, Villa Scarpariello, Pastificio Di Martino, Gennaro Esposito, Pasquale and Rafaella, Elvio Ruocco, Pino Lavarra at Rosellini's, Gino Sorbillo, Il Pastaio in Minori Bologna Family Giacobazzi, Giulia Gentile, Monica Luppi and all the ragazzi at San Patrignano, Casa Artusi, Vecchia Scuola Bolognese, Sara and Riccardo at Arcigay Piemonte Maria Nava & Piero Rondolino of Acquarello rice, Jean Leonard Touadi, San Secondo, Rettore Tanaro Maurizio Rasero, Vittorio Castellani aka Chef Kumalé PugliaSan Pio, Stefano Campanella of Tele Radio Padre Pio, Julie Cifaldi and Antonio Sienna of Voce di Padre Pio, I Frati Minori del Santuario di San Matteo, Carlo, Nicola & Dino of Masseria Calderosa, Angelo di Biccari of Pane e Salute, Comune di Orsara, Santuario di San Michele, Vincenza, Maria, Leonardo and Vito from Orsara, Michele del Giudice and the Comune di Foggia.

Editorial Director Jane O'Shea
Creative Director Helen Lewis
Project Editor Simon Davis
Designer Claire Peters
Photographer Chris Terry
Editor Susan Fleming
Food Stylist Anna Jones
Production Director Vincent Smith
Production Controller Marina Asenjo

First published in 2011 by
Quadrille Publishing Limited
Alhambra House
27–31 Charing Cross Road
London WC2H 0LS
www.quadrille.co.uk

This paperback edition first published in 2012

Text © 2011 Antonio Carluccio and Gennaro Contaldo
Photography © 2011 Chris Terry
Design and layout © 2011 Quadrille Publishing Ltd

Cataloguing in Publication Data: a catalogue record for this book is available from the British Library.

ISBN 978 184949 263 8

Printed in China

208